Sacred Home

Laurine Morrison Meyer has been a practicing interior designer for the past twenty-five years, focusing on creating homes imbued with a "soulful" quality supporting the physical and personal needs of the occupants. She was a professor and program coordinator for interior design at a Northern California college, and has taught summer courses abroad. She holds a bachelor's degree in psychology and a master's in interior design/education. Currently she divides her time between a home in the Sonoran Desert and a mountain retreat in the Northwest.

Sacred Home

Creating Shelter
for Your Soul

Laurine Morrison Meyer

Llewellyn Publications
St. Paul, Minnesota 55164-0383, U.S.A.

First Edition
Second Printing, 2004

Cover design by Lisa Novak
Cover photograph © 2004 Photodisc / Getty Images
Editing and interior design by Connie Hill
Interior art by Llewellyn Art Department
Tarot card images from *The Universal Tarot Deck* © Lo Scarabeo, used with permission.

Library of Congress Cataloging-in-Publication Data
Meyer, Laurine Morrison, 1942–.
  Sacred home : creating shelter for your soul / Laurine Morrison Meyer.
     p. cm.
  Includes bibliographical references and index.
  ISBN 0-7387-0585-3
  1. Home—Religious aspects. 2. Spiritual life. I. Title.
BL588.M49   2004   2004048771
204'.4—dc22

Llewellyn Publications
A Division of Llewellyn Worldwide, Ltd.
P.O. Box 64383, Dept. 0-7387-0585-3
St. Paul, MN 55164-0383, U.S.A.
www.llewellyn.com

Printed in the United States of America

Dedication

This book is dedicated to my family. To my oldest son Brad, whose creative genius fills me with awe and I pray will assist him through his "dark night of the soul." To my son, Darren, whose quest for spiritual truths has guided his path since he was a small child, and to his lovely and creative wife Alisa, who adds so much to our family. To my son Craig, who lights up a room and our lives with his positive and joyful attitude. To my daughter Darcy, who lives her convictions of a simple life without consumerism and magically transforms her family's environment with found objects, handmade items, and produce from her organic gardens. To my daughter Cherise, who has a natural talent for design and shares my passion for decorating and finding great buys at the flea market! To my stepson Tres and his wife Ericka, who enjoy decorating their special home together. To my stepdaughter Allison, intuitive and creative gardener, homemaker, busy wife, and mother. And to my loving and supportive husband Chuck, who has encouraged me to follow my own path every step of the way. Together we share a love of renovating neglected houses and creating soul-nurturing homes.

Contents

Part One: Historic Tour of Sacred Homes

	Introduction	3
Chapter 1	The Sacred Home	11
Chapter 2	Ancient Symbols of Home	21
Chapter 3	Household Deities	35
Chapter 4	Deities or Demons?	51
Chapter 5	Protecting the Sacred Home	67

Part Two: Creating Sacred Homes

Chapter 6	Essential Elements	85
Chapter 7	Archetypal Design Styles	101
Chapter 8	Calling Spirit Home	143
Chapter 9	Housewarming	157
Chapter 10	Propitious Principles	181
Chapter 11	Auspicious Symbols	203
Chapter 12	The Enchanted Dwelling	227
	Bibliography	235
	Suggested Reading	239
	Index	241

PART ONE

Historic Tour of Sacred Homes

Introduction

Is there a Western equivalent to the Eastern practice of
Feng Shui? Did we in the West, at any time in history,
believe that our homes could bring good fortune if we
used special icons, performed certain rituals, aligned
the house and furnishings in specific ways for optimal
energy flow, and listened to the spirits of place? Within our own cultural lineage is there evidence that at
one time our homes were considered sacred? Are there
energies or spirits that inhabit this space? Are good
luck charms of past generations silly superstitions, or
is there any historical precedent for their widespread
usage? Is there a common basis for the almost universal
use of certain symbols found in and around the home?
If so, how is any of this meaningful to us today?

Curious about the answers to these questions, I
began research for this particular book about six years

ago—but I have to say that most of my life has been leading up to writing it. Spiritually curious since a child, I've studied, dabbled, and tried on various religious disciplines over the last fifty-some years. As far as homes go, I've always been fascinated with them; especially those that need TLC—fixer-uppers. I guess I have what might be described as a certain intuitive sense about houses. Sometimes I feel very strongly drawn or repelled by certain ones. I take a keen interest in the psychology of personal space, drawing on my undergraduate degree in psychology and graduate degree in interior design—and I've spent the past twenty-five years studying, practicing, and teaching that discipline.

During my teaching career, I taught students to recognize distinguishing characteristics in architecture, furnishings, and interior decorative motifs of various cultures believed to be the dominant influences in the development of contemporary architectural and interior styles. I could enumerate these identifying symbols and patterns, but I never thought to question what they meant, or even if there was a meaning, other than corresponding to political and social events, or simply current fashion. Their more arcane symbolic meanings were left unquestioned.

A number of years ago, while taking an art history course in Florence, Italy, I became fascinated with the symbols depicted in the religious art of the medieval and Renaissance eras. There seemed to be a secret, unspoken language, a kind of esoteric code. I knew the translations of the more obvious Christian symbolism, but I was curious about the exotic ones whose origins were unexplained, or those synonymous with pagan symbols. Certain flowers, trees, fruits, birds, animals, and shapes appeared in various works of art, almost reaching out of the picture trying to relate some secret message to the viewer. Among the most fascinating to me were those symbols associated with classical mythological characters, but incorporated into Christian images of the Virgin Mary. The pomegranate, the crescent moon, the dove, stars, lilies, and so many other symbols are found in the iconography of many cultures, not just Christian ones. They whispered to me of universal origins. Why was Mary depicted with a crescent moon and stars on her robe like the Egyptian goddesses Maat, or the Bronze Age goddess, Inanna, who was also known as the Queen of Heaven?[1] Why the lily or the pomegranate? Where did the symbol of the dove originate? What about the horseshoe-shaped thresholds under which Mary was so often portrayed?

While teaching an interior design course in Paris one summer, I was researching medieval furniture in the Cluny Museum. The museum itself is built over Roman ruins almost 2,000 years old, and displays an unusually broad range of artifacts: Marovingian jewels, medieval tapestries, stone heads of Christian prophets (thought to be kings; decapitated from Notre Dame Cathedral during the French Revolution), and a wonderful Celtic pillar, to name just a few. Because of the museum's wide array of artifacts, I was again struck by the repetition, throughout history and across thousands of miles, of elusive symbols carrying some type of hidden message. From then on, wherever I went: Gothic cathedrals, museums, Renaissance chateaus, ancient castles, these esoteric symbols filled my mind with questions. Why did Napoleon favor the symbol of the bee? What did the fleur-de-lis signify, and why was it often portrayed as three flowers in a triangular shape? And what made that particular flower so remarkable that it represented a long line of French rulers?

Again, as I began researching this book, gathering information about various household good luck charms, I was amazed at not only the cross-cultural similarities but also the contradictory meanings given by supposed authoritative sources. Symbols that meant good luck could also be bad luck if turned in the wrong direction. Left and right, sun and moon, hands and eyes all took on virtuous and evil meanings depending upon the source. Why was the snake so reviled—a guise of Satan himself, yet considered by many cultures to be a venerated household guardian? Why was it unlucky to circle to the left, but circling to the left was common in ancient folk dances in many parts of Europe? The ubiquitous horseshoe over the door; some sources claimed it was only lucky if its ends pointed up lest the luck run out; others claimed the opposite. Where did the symbol of the horseshoe originate? Why was it lucky? Which way should it hang? These questions and many others led me back further and further in history. The same horseshoe shape is venerated as threshold profiles throughout the Muslim world and in ancient India. What did this shape originally signify?

My research became labyrinthine. Sometimes I felt as if I were going in circles searching for the elusive meaning of a particular icon; often I came to dead ends. Just researching the meaning of the fleur-de-lis for example, I found it had been the topic of vigorous discussion for hundreds of years. Why and when did this symbol become associated with the kings of France? Was it a lily or an iris? Since the iris was associated with a Roman goddess (the messenger of the gods) this wouldn't do for a Christian king. Some medieval Christian dogma asserts that the motif was given directly by the Virgin Mary to Clovis (an early French king) to replace the pagan symbol he previously used. Some say his original symbol was the triple crescent moon. Other sources claim that Clovis used a triangular symbol of three toads, and that it was the actual precursor of the fleur-de-lis.[2] The fleur-de-lis was also an important symbol in such far-reaching cultures as Egypt, Japan, China, Assyria, and Mesopotamia. It was the widespread use of certain revered symbols from very disparate regions that led to questions concerning their origin.

I also recognized throughout my design career that some homes exhibited a certain trait, something that was not taught—an elusive attribute that made a home literally dance with vitality—a welcoming quality that had something to do with light and color and the occupants of the home, but it was also something quite indescribable. This book represents my research and my own observations over a twenty-five-year period of analyzing homes and that mysterious quality that sets some of them apart. I present this material with the hope that it will make a difference in the way we regard our homes, and if we do, I firmly believe our homes will repay us many times over.

This is my second manuscript for this book. Four years ago, after a good deal of work, I put the original away. At that time, my life took a downward spiral to the very depths of Hell itself. As I watched in abject terror, my oldest son was arrested, placed on trial, and sentenced to life in prison. I was a mother living her worst nightmare. My pain and grief for my son and the others involved in the tragic incident were unfathomable. Fortunately my deep abiding belief in a Higher Power and the close relationship I had developed with my Spiritual Guides, along with my personal spiritual practices, kept me from drowning in sorrow. I created new areas of sanctuary in my home. Symbols and rituals took on deeper meanings. The religious and mythological archetypes of mother and son took on deep personal meaning. I began a new journey of self-discovery. Last spring I decided to do something with the original manuscript. I took it out and reread it—it felt sweet and superficial. I had changed so much during those few years. I knew I would need to rewrite much of the original manuscript. What I didn't know was that I would rewrite the entire book. As I rewrote, I often felt it had a life of its own; as if someone else was writing through me—someone who sincerely wanted this story told. I thank her for the loving guidance she has freely given me during the writing of this book; and I in no way blame her for my inadequacies as a writer.

---

1 Kris Waldherr, *The Book of Goddesses*, Hillsboro, OR: Beyond Words Publishing.

2 Claudia De Lys, *A Treasury of American Superstitions*, New York: Philosophical Library, 139.

Chapter 1

The Sacred Home

. . . a dwelling is truly a sacred space. I don't
mean this romantically or fantastically, but I
think there is a kind of spirit, an inherent
sacredness, within a home . . .

Thomas Moore[1]

The Spirit of Place

Have you ever been in a home where everything felt
vibrantly alive? A place where colors and light literally
sparkled and you yearned to prolong your stay? The
harmonious surroundings reflected the personalities of
the occupants, adding a richness of character. You recall the ambiance as comfortable and nurturing, combined with an almost sacred quality that set it apart
from other, more mundane homes. It was probably
not the most elaborate setting that you've been in, but
a certain quality held your attention and kept you
thinking about the space long after you were gone.

In contrast, I recall a house I designed a number of years ago for a successful young couple. Everything in the home was newly purchased, nothing taken from previous houses. After the home was furnished and decorated I waited several months to have a professional photographer take pictures for my portfolio. What a surprise when I returned to find everything exactly as I left it. The home was beautifully coordinated with exquisite furniture and accessories, but it felt dead. I quickly visited a florist and bought some potted plants and flowers to add life. When I asked the owners for personal items to display, they looked dismayed and said they didn't have anything appropriate. What a lesson for me early in my career. Their house felt like a model home, pretty to look at, but sterile and lifeless. There was no sense of the owners. Who were they and what did they hold sacred?

Personal Style

At its most fulfilling, your home will feel alive. It will be a reflection of your own unique tastes and a true expression of your inner essence. Colors, patterns, and furnishings will be well balanced and appropriately selected for the function of the space, but also, and very importantly, they will express the interests, personal needs, and preferences of you, the owner. If the home or living space is shared by more than one person, then each occupant should have a voice in the final selections. If possible, each individual residing in the home should have an area that is a personal reflection of that individual. Never let someone tell you that your home must match the designer's preconceived idea of good taste. On the other hand, if your own style is a hodge-podge of various themes, you will probably feel more satisfied with the overall effect if there is some relationship and agreement among parts. Nature uses a wide variety of colors and textures, but seasons and geographical locations contribute to natural overall themes. For example, a cactus in an English garden is not as appropriate as it is in a desert landscape; neither are combinations of delicate summer flowers in a bouquet of winter evergreens. The same holds true for various interior styles. In chapter 7 I will acquaint you with four basic archetypes of design. These archetypes will simplify and condense design choices to help you identify your own personal style.

Does your own home represent who you are? How do you feel when you walk into your home? Does it welcome you? Does it have a harmonious and unique character?

Sacred Dwellings

There is another essential ingredient that needs inclusion if we wish our homes to have the unforgettable quality mentioned above. This elusive essence that brings a house to life is sometimes referred to as *the spirit of place*, the crucial energy that gives added dimension to our homes. When we furnish houses strictly for the function of the bodies that will inhabit them, or to create a certain style, we lose touch with this vital animating principle. To create a home that feels spiritually alive, we must be mindful of our deepest thoughts and feelings, our connection to wise elders and ancestors, and what it is that lies at the very center of our beings. We must find out what it is that will make our hearts and spirits joyful!

Today, we often downplay the importance of our homes. In doing so, we fail to develop environments that support our mental, emotional, physical, and spiritual well-being. Instead we spend our time and money on high-tech appliances and elaborate electronic paraphernalia that numb our minds and consume our time. Many of us have forgotten that, for much of recorded history, homes were treated quite differently than they are today. They were considered sacred. Certainly, we recognize that our most basic and essential activities: procreation, nourishment, and rest, take place here, but before spiritual practice was taken from the realms of the common people and placed in the domain of priests, monks, and ministers, it was common practice in cultures throughout the world to acknowledge and revere household deities, and to respect and honor the home as a sacred space. Spirituality was part of everyday life, not just reserved for the hours of the Sabbath. Each home was protected by totems, deities, ancestors, or spirits that were honored by the family and in turn gave a sense of spiritual protection to the inhabitants. From primitive earth-based animism to highly structured formal religions, we find historical evidence of the acknowledgement of the spirits of place, the *genii loci*, who live among mortals on the earth plane. Shrines were maintained and given honored placement in the home. Protective amulets were installed in strategic places, and rituals were practiced to purify and consecrate the sanctity of the home. When the home is treated as sacred, a numinous vitality emerges. The home becomes a living entity that interacts with our essential being.

Do you treat your home reverently as a sacred space? Does your home contain spiritual artifacts? Are your accessories personally meaningful, or just quickly selected to fill space or match the decor?

Sacred Symbols

Our homes are filled with symbolic meaning. We may or may not have intentionally selected the symbols that are evident in our homes, but subliminally they are sending messages. Most patterns are based on historic symbols with sacred meanings that were well known and openly acknowledged in previous times. Without understanding the meaning of the symbols we may be subconsciously saying things to ourselves and others that are not intentional, perhaps even diametrically opposed to our own personal beliefs.

Symbols form a mystical language associated with sacred images, folklore, and classical mythic tales. Bent and refigured over time, sometimes reversed, but recognizable as having deeper, coded meanings, they reflect our sacred relationship to home. From the earliest dwellings of primitive beings, symbols passed from one generation to the next—so sacred that they were remembered for thousands of years, and surround us still. They are so imbedded in our psyche that we sometimes intuitively feel we are separated from some deeper meaning that we can't quite grasp. We might even feel a vague and persistent loneliness, a longing for something lost, something important. We are disconnected from the sacred nature of everyday life and have misplaced the keys to the secret garden. We spend our time searching for meaning in a world filled with apparent chaos, alienated from the teachings of our elders, believing their stories to be nothing more than primitive superstitions. We are turned out into the vast desolate landscape known in mythology as the barren desert, "starved for ritual that reifies our connection to the sacred source of our being."[2] It's no wonder we feel distanced from our sacred lineage.

As you look around your home, what symbols do you see? Look at the patterns in your fabrics and accessories. Do you know their meanings? Do you feel connected to your ancient heritage?

Feng Shui

In recent years, Feng Shui, the ancient Chinese practice of favorable energy alignment in designing and situating dwellings, has become popular. Many Westerners have adopted these principles, hoping to create more spiritual environments. Although the purpose is venerated, some have found it awkward to follow advice that feels foreign to their own aesthetic tastes. Colors, for instance, have different connotations depending upon cultural associations. Whereas red is considered a sign of good luck in China, in Western cultures red is often associated with prostitution, passion, and fast food eateries. Auspicious placement and choice of accessories and protective icons also vary from one culture to the next. For instance, in Roman times, it was customary to position the household shrine, called the *Lararium*, opposite the entry door so it was the first thing seen upon entering the home. The hearth, along with the appropriate protective goddess, was the very heart of the home. The doors and thresholds held such importance that more than six gods and goddesses and countless amulets and rituals are associated with them.

Western Cultural Traditions

With the spread of the Roman Empire, ancient spiritual practices were scattered throughout the Western world. The conquering army's gods, goddesses, and customs merged with and replaced some of those of the conquered. This amalgamation of deities and symbolism passing from one generation to the next, gathering local color and embellishment, became the rich body of folklore that was cherished and protected long after its worship was no longer permitted.

Somewhere, deep within us, we long to reconnect with this sacred heritage. Although many of the details have been forgotten, the symbols and bits and pieces of ancient rituals remind us of forgotten aspects of ourselves. This is the yarn that is woven into our collective unconscious—this bond of belonging to a broader community with all the beliefs, customs, and spirituality that add dimension to our lives. Subconsciously we realize that something is missing in our contemporary homes. Perhaps the threads that connect us to our ancestors are yearning to be reconnected.

When we incorporate the myths, symbols, folklore, and other aspects of our unique history in designing our life space, we create personalized spiritual environments—much more satisfying than merely imitating someone else's style. We reconnect with our own personal spiritual nature, our sacred ancient heritage. By recognizing that symbols and myths are not just vague fears of a superstitious primitive people, but represent a reverence and respect for the miraculous forces of nature, we can reactivate our numinous relationship to our own homes, respectfully aware of the spirits that guard and protect us.

Do you feel a longing to reconnect with your own heritage? What elements are incorporated in your home that serve to connect you with your own heritage?

---

1 Thomas Moore, *Handbook for the Soul*, edited by Richard Carlson and Benjamin Shield, Little Brown & Co., 1995, 26.

2 Elinor W. Gadon, *The Once and Future Goddess*, New York: HarperCollins Publishers, 1989, 227.

Chapter 2

Ancient Symbols of Home

The first, real sacred spaces were probably
caves in southern France and northern Spain,
dating from 30,000 BC.[1]

Joseph Campbell

The Original Symbols of Home

Sometimes we confuse ancient spiritual beliefs with
superstitions, and scoff at our ancestral folklore as
nothing more than primitive thinking. We have also
been told that many symbols have evil connotations;
and we are reluctant to use them due to subtle, but
deeply ingrained, fears. In this chapter, as we take a
brief but more ancient look at symbols associated with
the home, we will uncover lost meanings that have been
buried through centuries of intense religious purging.

When we learn that our ancestors believed in the oneness of all life and held a deep, sacred connection with nature and the earth, we will understand that rather than being evil or repugnant, the earliest symbols represent a reverence for the magic of life, and a love and respect for the First Mother and our earthly home.

Artifacts found by archeologists in the earliest human shelters speak of the ancient people's veneration of the home as sacred space. Many anthropologists believe the cave and later tent and round house were symbolically thought of as the womb of the Great Mother. In fact, the earliest known language, Sanskrit, uses the same word for temple as it does for womb. The name of the ancient oracle shrine in Greece, Delphi, also means womb.[2] Just as the womb houses, protects, and nourishes the unborn child, our homes house, nourish, and protect us. The house was a metaphor for the womb of the earth: the first Mother who gave birth to all life and took all life back into her womb at death, only to resurrect it into new life.

According to archeologist Marija Gimbutas, symbols depicting the reproductive areas of the female anatomy were among the earliest forms of decoration.[3] One of the most awesome examples is the Goddess of Laussel carved over the opening to a Paleolithic cave in southern France and believed to have been executed over 25,000 years ago! In one hand she holds a bison horn, while the other hand points to her pubic triangle. She is a symbol of the shelter that she protects: the sacred dwelling where the creation of life itself took place.

The primordial birthing mother was as awesome and powerful as anything the early tribe could imagine. Out of a narrow passage, accompanied with miraculous, life-sustaining fluids, she produced her own miniature replica. She was completely capable of creating more fluids from her breasts; perfect nourishment for the newly born infant. This mystical life-producing female became venerated as the physical representation of the Great Mother Goddess. Her magical body was honored, replicas of her form painstakingly scraped with crude instruments onto entryways and artifacts; emphasis placed on her most sacred aspects.

Symbols of the reproductive areas of female anatomy became stylized and reproduced in myriad forms over the next several thousand years on pottery, votive figures, on walls in homes and temples, vases, figurines, musical instruments, ritual objects, furnishings, and almost every imaginable article associated with shelter and religion.

Triangles and Vs [fig. 1] are ancient symbols originally representing the female pubic area. Wavy or straight lines indicated vitalizing fluids produced by the female; mounds and circles symbolize her pregnant belly and enlarged breasts [fig. 2].[4] The vulva, vagina, and womb shapes were replicated thousands of times in

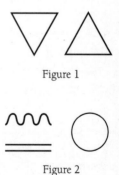

Figure 1

Figure 2

art and ritualistic instruments. Ovals, pointed ovals, almond shapes, and cowrie shells [fig. 3] represent the vulva; the circle and Greek Omega shapes are symbolic of the womb [fig. 4]. Even to the present day, we use a representation of the womb in the form of a horseshoe as a protective amulet over our doors! Another interesting symbol that has been repeated for thousands of years is the ancient symbol of home and hearth, a circle with a dot in the center; originally representing the belly with navel or the breast of the birthing mother, in later history it became a symbol for the sun and air and the all-seeing-eye (also depicted as a pointed oval with a dot in the middle [fig. 5]).

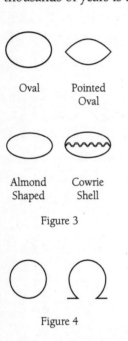

Oval   Pointed
            Oval

Almond   Cowrie
Shaped   Shell

Figure 3

Figure 4

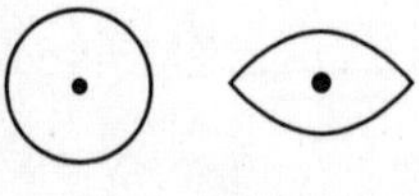

Figure 5

As you look around your own home, how many symbols do you see that are symbolic of female anatomy? Look at the patterns on textiles, rugs, ceramics, and other artifacts in magazines, or when touring museums. You'll be amazed at the quantity of symbols representing a woman's reproductive parts that have been drawn and woven into our homes.

The First Altar

Fire was magical and sacred to our ancestors. The fire pit in the center of the dwelling has been synonymous with the fire of life in the womb of the Universal Mother since prehistoric time.[5] In fact, the family hearth was considered the original altar. It was revered for thousands of years as a sacred space, long before more formal altars were placed in church buildings. Later, during the Roman Empire, every household hearth was dedicated to the goddess of domestic and ceremonial fire, Vesta, the Roman equivalent of the Greek goddess Hestia. Their temples were round, with a sacred fire in the center, the primal shape associated with the fire of life inside the Mother's womb.

Fire was considered sacred life energy and had an integral relationship with the home. In ancient Rome, when a couple or family moved from their home to a new residence, they would bring burning coals from the ancestral hearth to light the first fire in their new household. This symbolic act was a ritual performed to bless and honor the sacred spirit of home and to bring a spark of the vital life force from their old home into the new one. Housewarming rituals still remembered and practiced in many parts of the world today carry vestiges of these early rites.

In Ireland it was the goddess Brigit (Brigid, Brighid, Brigantia, Bride) who protected the home and hearth. A perpetual flame in her temple, tended by dedicated priestesses, and later by nuns, was kept alight for over a thousand years, until the thirteenth century CE when a local bishop, deeming the fire-tending rites to be pagan, demanded that the fire be extinguished.[6] "Under Brigid's mantle" means, "May you be safe and warm," a common blessing still used today when people travel from their Irish home.

The hearth is represented in pictorial form as two upright columns with a horizontal line over the top, also a symbol for the altar and the Pi or opening into the sacred dwelling or womb. The symbol of the goddess Vesta is the symbol Pi (altar or hearth) with an inverted uterus shape on top, also known as horns or flames [fig. 6].

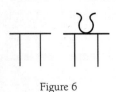

Figure 6

The Horn and Crescent Moon

The horn shape as we witnessed in the hand of the Goddess of Laussel is an ancient symbol linked to the earliest goddess figures; it's most common association is the horn of plenty, symbol of nourishing abundance. The horn is also associated with the crescent-shaped moon, symbolic of growth and regeneration.[7] In ancient mythology the horn and the crescent moon were depicted as receptacles of menstrual blood with which each mother formed the life of her child. "The crescent moon worn by Diana and used in the worship of other Goddesses is said to be the Ark or vessel of boat-like shape, symbol of fertility or the Container of the Germ of all life [fig. 7]."[8]

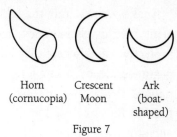

Horn (cornucopia)   Crescent Moon   Ark (boat-shaped)

Figure 7

In a classical story the Greek god Zeus, was nursed by a goat, whose horn became known as the cornucopia or horn of plenty, referring to the horn's symbolic meaning as a container filled with life-sustaining nourishment.[9]

In our homes, the horn of plenty is associated with the harvest and the abundant fruits of nature. Have you used this symbol for Thanksgiving celebrations yourself? The horn and crescent moon are further simplified and incorporated in patterns as half circles. When fertility or abundance is desired, bringing this symbol into your home can be very auspicious.

The Serpent

The snake is almost universally known in folklore as a protective household ancestor or domestic spirit, suggesting its very ancient origins. It is symbolized as a coil, spiral, or vertical coiling shape, often wrapped around a pole or tree [fig. 8]. It has been reproduced as symbols on painted pottery and artifacts for over 7,000 years.[10]

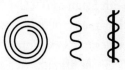

Figure 8

Snakes were surely the early cohabitants with ancient cave dwellers. They made their dens in dark protective caves where they laid coiled, and for all appearances dead, during long months of winter hibernation. Maybe they even shared a deep recess in the back of the cave used as a burial place for deceased ancestors. After months of inertia, the snakes miraculously returned to life with the onset of warm weather. Widely believed to contain the souls of dead ancestors, it's not hard to see where that idea may have originated.

Their strong sinuous movements climbing trees or swimming, seemingly without effort, the shedding of skins and their miraculous ability to come back from the dead, became symbolic of vital life energy, renewal, and rebirth.

The snake might also have represented the umbilical cord as the source of vital life energy bringing nourishment to the new life inside the womb.

Over time, these symbols and beliefs became woven into the folklore of Western cultures and maintained even today in countries such as Ireland and Lithuania. Unfortunately, the serpent became demonized with the onset of patriarchal religions and the association with Satan in the Garden of Eden. The unfounded fear that many people have of snakes is due to the centuries of its evil implications.

Snake artifacts are wonderful protective amulets in your home. Do you have patterns with wavy lines or spirals? You might be surprised at the snake symbols already in your home.

Birds

Female votive figures with aspects of bird's features have been used in house shrines since the Early Neolithic period. These figures were often endowed with breasts and wings, sometimes with beaks or bird heads. Birds, like snakes, were considered household guardians. Birds were thought to contain the souls of departed ancestors and were symbolic of divine wisdom. They wisely oversaw the well-being and health of the family and provided protection as well as additions to the food supply.[11]

In folklore, witches and fairies are often portrayed with bird or chicken feet like the Russian house spirit *Kikimora* and the Lithuanian fairies, the *Laumes*.

The Irish *Imbolc*, a celebration of the goddess Brigit, is a fire-centered ritual ending in a search for bird or chicken tracks in the morning-after ashes. If bird tracks are found it is a sign of good fortune—the goddess has visited.

In ancient Egypt, the goddess Nekhebet (worshipped in Nekheb, the oldest settlement of Egypt[12]) is portrayed as a vulture. She became the symbol of Upper Egypt and was worn on the king's headdress just as the cobra represented Lower (Northern) Egypt. Nekhebet, like the prehistoric Bird Goddess, is associated with nurturing (as the breasts on ancient bird/woman figures indicate) and is seen in wall murals suckling the royal child and even the king himself.[13]

The V is used as an abstraction and common decorative motif relating to the bird aspect of the Goddess. As previously mentioned, the V has its earliest association with the female pubic area. According to noted historical researcher Claudia De Lys, "The letters V and U at one time were interchangeable and both symbolic of the crotch, the source of life."[14] Other closely related symbols are meandering Vs, zigzags, two inverted Vs (the shape of the Greek symbol Mu), and the X motif formed when the two Vs connect in the middle [fig. 9]. Ritual vessels of the bird goddess were decorated with these geometric variations and with the hourglass and butterfly or bee motif: two triangles connected at the apex [fig. 10]. The bird goddess was most likely venerated as the ancient ancestress of the family.

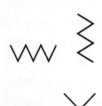

Figure 9

The symbols for bees and butterflies are closely related to those of the bird. Bees symbolize a woman's ability to produce food from her own body, and the hive is similar to the shape and function of her womb. Milk and honey are often paired in mythology as the elixir of the gods. The bee-hive is an attribute of the Earth

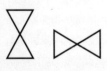

Figure 10

Goddess as Demeter and is closely associated with the moon. In the home, bees symbolize abundant food and protective shelter.

When you think of the strange and seemingly magical existence of a caterpillar who forms a cocoon (womb-like) and later, instead of dying, emerges as a totally different entity, a beautiful butterfly, you can understand why this small insect is a universal symbol of transformation. The stylized symbol of the butterfly, two triangles joined at their apex in the middle [fig. 10], appears throughout history. This same motif also symbolizes the double axe often carried by goddess figures in later European mythology, and the female form itself. The Greek goddess Hera, known as the Holy Mother, wore a golden double axe between her sacred horns.[15]

Bird and bee symbols have wonderful, time-honored guardian attributes used in the home. Since birds are thought to contain the souls and thus the wisdom of deceased ancestors, they represent the wise direction of revered elders, and add a soulful quality to our homes. Bees symbolize protective shelter (the hive) and an abundant food supply (honey) for the family. The butterfly is indicative of physical and spiritual transformation, and we are reminded of the continuing cycle of all life. Many geometric patterns are variations of the V and X and joined triangles. Look around you and see if you can identify any bird, bee, or butterfly symbols on patterns in your home. The next time you're out walking where birds have been feeding on soft ground, notice the shape of their tracks.

Mother Nature

From observing nature, our ancestors noted the similarities of the larger ecosystem to the form and functions of the human reproductive cycle. The entire earth itself became symbolic of the body of the Divine Feminine from which all things are born. Water, flowers, trees, caves, and mounds of earth were seen as archetypal places of mythical birth.

After the introduction of agriculture, rituals were created to invoke the blessings of the Earth Mother to ensure abundant harvest. She who could create food from her own body was worshipped and prayed to for favorable conditions to germinate the seeds and bring water from the sky (Cow goddess) to irrigate the crops. The metaphor of earth as a feminine being is almost universally found in ancient myths. Roman philosophers believed that the Earth Mother was the mysterious power that awakened everything to life, as well as the great recycler who took life into her womb and transformed it.[16]

Spirituality was immanent, a part of everyday life for these ancient people. As careful observers of nature, our ancestors recognized the cycles of birth, growth, death, and regeneration. All of nature is recycled. Nothing vanishes. Life forms transform into other life forms. Tadpoles transform into frogs, caterpillars into butterflies, eggs into birds and snakes. Dead animals and humans are eaten by insects, birds, and other animals.

The dead do not remain inert, but are transformed into the body of the living.

If one observes nature closely enough he/she will recognize that everything in nature is nourishment for everything else, and does indeed transform into something else. From the simplest life form to the most complex, all life is food for other life—all is recycled, nothing is exempt. Our ancestors witnessed the earth as a living entity and all beings as part of her. They worshipped her in all aspects: life giver, nourisher, death wielder, and regenetrix. She represented the natural cycles of birth, maturation, death, and regeneration. Symbolized by the sacred triangle from earliest history [fig. 1], She became known as the triple Goddess: maiden, mother, and crone.

To summarize, the earliest known religion was home based and included veneration for the reproductive capacities of the female. Symbolically this veneration extended to include all of nature: insects, birds, fish, and animals represented cycles of birth, nourishment, death, and rebirth. The earth itself was seen as the Great Mother, and our earliest homes: caves, tents, and later sun-baked brick houses, were symbolic of her sacred womb—the sacrosanct place that sheltered and nourished new life, the center of which was the hearth (both heart and earth are contained in this word), the first altar. The first ancient earthly temple, considered the most sacred of all space, was the home.

When you think of your home as a descendent of the first sacred temple, do you see it in a more revered light? How do you show reverence and respect to this symbolic aspect of the Divine Mother?

---

1 Diane K. Osbon, *Reflections on the Art of Living; A Joseph Campbell Companion,* New York: HarperCollins Publishers, 1991, 186.

2 Barbara Walker, *The Woman's Dictionary of Symbols and Sacred Objects,* New York: HarperCollins Publishers, 1988, 330.

3 Marija Gimbutas, *The Language of the Goddess,* New York: Harper-Collins Publishers, 1991 ed., 3.

4 Gimbutas, xxii, 3.

5 Campbell, *Hero With a Thousand Faces,* Princeton, NJ: Princeton University Press, 1968 ed., 42.

6 Merlin Stone, *Ancient Mirrors of Womanhood,* Boston: Beacon Press, 1990 ed., 65.

7 J. C. Cooper, *An Illustrated Encyclopedia of Traditional Symbols,* London: Thames and Hudson, 1978, 107.

8 Gadon, 671.

9 Michael Macrone, *By Jove! Brush Up Your Mythology,* New York: HarperCollins Publishers, 1992, 182.

10 Gimbutas, 121.

11 Ibid, 317.

12 Clive Barrett, *The Egyptian Gods and Goddesses,* London: Diamond Books, 1996, 95.

13 Ibid, 95.

14 Claudia De Lys, *A Treasury of American Superstitions,* New York: Philosophical Library Inc., 1948, 442.

15 Stone, *Ancient Mirrors,* 373.

16 Barbara Walker, *The Woman's Encyclopedia of Myths and Secrets,* New York: HarperCollins Publishers, 1983, 264.

Chapter 3

Household Deities

In ancient times [sic] there was an altar in
every room of the home. The home was where
spirit lived . . .[1]

Tsultrim Allione; Sky Dancer

The Arrival of the Sky Gods

As we follow the historical path of this ancient female
and earth-centered religion and its symbols, even after
thousands of years of political conquests and religious
abolition, we can still recognize remnants woven
throughout Western culture. As we know from American history, we are taught the truths of past events
from the viewpoint of the conquerors. What we have
been told were quaint superstitions and pagan beliefs
of illiterate people were, in actuality, profound and surprisingly contemporary logic about the interrelated-
ness and oneness of all things. The ancient belief that

the earth was a living entity likened to the Original Mother, and that all beings were her children, is now assuming a more scientific basis. Discoveries in quantum physics and mechanics over the last century have clearly shown that everything is composed of vibratory energy; the living as well as the nonliving, and that our bodies and our physical surroundings at the subatomic level are all made up of tiny packets of light energy continually interacting with each other. In essence, we are all one; inseparable from our surrounding environment, the earth itself! Separation and dualistic thinking that pits one faction against another was imposed by invaders and subsequent rulers of these primal, peace-loving societies. Even though the ancient worship of the original Mother was systematically exterminated, we are still able to find vestiges of its practice in our homes today. As we look at the evolution of the sacred home and the icons and symbols that were used to consecrate it, we will see where many fearful misconceptions have arisen. This will help to dispel fears and superstitions that have been deeply ingrained in the collective consciousness for millennia.

The Path of the Goddess

For thousands of years the indigenous people of old Europe lived in relative peace, worshipping female deities and using a matrilineal form of property transfer. They created agriculture, weaving, pottery making, and developed highly sophisticated houses with plumbing and built-in furnishings. It wasn't until the arrival of bands of warring tribes around 4300 BCE that evidence of weapons is found. These conquering tribes of Indo-Europeans were domesticators of sheep and cattle who came on horseback and in chariots, searching for new grazing land for their herds. These invasions took place in several waves over a 1,500-year span.[2,3,4]

Many historians claim the time period marked by the arrival of the Indo-European tribes to be the "beginning of recorded history." This is patently untrue. Civilizations such as Catalhoyuk in western Turkey were highly evolved cultures; and they predate the arrival of these conquering bands by at least a thousand years.

Eventually the conquerors imposed a patriarchal ruling hierarchy and introduced their own gods: Sky gods associated with the sun, lightning, and thunderbolts. Their myths tell of conquests and victories, of great warrior heroes who became the gods, of the dominance of the sun over the moon, and the power of the sun's heat to dry up the waters of the earth.

Dominating the Goddess

Classical mythology becomes more understandable when we acknowledge the archeological evidence that a previous matrilineal goddess-worshipping culture existed in Old Europe for thousands of years, and that at a particular point in history warring tribes who worshipped a patriarchal sky god overcame and eventually dominated these indigenous peoples.

These early recorded myths tell of ruling father gods, of intrigues, romantic interludes, triumphs and power, but they also allude to a more ancient female deity. Jove (Jupiter), the Roman father god, ruled the heavens and was master of storms, thunder, and lightning, but we know he was neither the oldest god nor the creator god. He was the one who put an end to a series of chaotic wars. In other words, he was the final victor.[5] Juno, once known as the great goddess, protector of women and children, whose name was synonymous with a woman's soul, became his wife, but for centuries women had prayed to Juno as they would to their own soul or higher power. One of Juno's temples was even a sanctuary for abused women.[6] Later the name for a woman's soul was expunged and, depending upon the time in history, she was either allowed to share the man's soul (*genius*), or she was deprived of a soul altogether.[7]

Teutonic mythology recalls these invasions as the war between the Aesirs and the Vanirs. The Aesirs were the gods who came from the east and waged war on the more peace-loving gods, the Vanirs. Freya (Frigg, Frigga, Freyja) was a much older goddess, the ruling ancestress of the Disir or the divine grandmothers.[8]

In Egypt, followers of the male sun god Ra were the first to bring Upper and Lower Egypt together under the auspices of one pharaoh. From that time on, the sun, personified as Ra, became associated with the supreme ruler of Egypt. However, in predynastic times, Mut was known as the great and divine Mother. She was later designated as the mother of Ra.

In ancient Greece the earth goddess Gaea, the mother of all gods, slowly slipped into the background as the sky gods took center stage. Zeus, her grandson born of her children Rhea and Cronus, eventually evolved into the father god. He was even given the ability to reproduce, once believed to be the exclusive area of women! Athena was born from his head, and the rest is history. Unlike the female deities who were intimately involved in daily life on earth, the new gods are more distantly removed, somewhere up in the sky. Rather than a freely bestowed motherly love, the new gods were authoritarian and judgmental, exacting punishments and reserving reward for a later afterlife.[9]

Male Reproductive Role

Many of the traditional symbols of fertility and nurturing aspects of the Goddess eventually became signs of male virility. The Moon Goddess often appeared in ancient iconography as the Divine Cow, horned like the moon.[10] The cow and bison horns that historically represented the crescent moon and the fertile nurturing aspect of the Goddess became associated with the male reproductive role. Zeus became known as the Bull, consort of Hera (Europa, Io), the white Moon Cow, and was soon followed by almost all gods of the ancient

world, who at one time or another adopted aspects of
the bull.[11]

The snake also took on dual and mixed meanings
in classical mythology. The snake as a phallic symbol
became well-known in later mythology. Alexander the
Great was said to be sired by a god who impregnated
his mother, Queen Olympias, while in the form of a
serpent.[12]

But the serpent, long associated with Goddess worship, was also portrayed as an evil enemy that needed
to be curtailed or destroyed. For thousands of years in
Crete the snake was venerated as a household protector and reincarnated ancestor. Snakes were allowed to
travel through Cretan houses in special tubes made
specifically for that purpose,[13] and in certain ancient
goddess centers, such as the oracle at Delphi, snakes
were used for divination purposes. Because of their
use in divination, snakes were known as the eye of
wisdom (later demonized as the "Evil Eye").

When sacred Goddess temples were taken over and
looted by the new rulers, the decimations were recorded as triumphs. In Greek mythology the sun god Apollo was said to have won over the forces of darkness by
slaying the python and burying the beast under a rock
known as the navel or center of the world—mythological language for the suppression of Goddess worship
at the holy site of Delphi, long known as the navel and
womb of the Mother. This site on Mount Parnassus
then became the home of the mighty Apollo. These

examples of what mythology claimed as the triumph of light over darkness are just a sampling of the hundreds of recorded myths that associate the worship of feminine deities as dark and evil, while portraying male gods as righteous and all-powerful.

The Kings

At first, the new rulers borrowed the symbols of the Old Religion to give credence to their authority to rule. In Sumeria, the new kings claimed to be consorts of the Goddess Innana, thus giving them legal rights to the throne.

In Egypt, pharaohs wore symbols of the goddess on their heads to show their legitimacy. Isis was symbolized as the throne itself, which was also the hieroglyph of her name.[14] Both the serpent in the form of a cobra representing the goddess of Lower Egypt, Udjat, and the vulture, symbol of Nekhebet, goddess of Upper Egypt, were worn by gods and pharaohs as symbols of their legitimate rule.[15]

The sky gods in their physical aspect as king or pharaoh ruled the people and their countries, gathering more and more land under their dominion. As they gained power, these conquering tribes gradually replaced the goddesses of the temples with their own versions of the gods who eventually became the approved religion of the state.

The Goddess as Guardian of the Home and Family

Eradicating the worship of a female deity did not happen easily. Because this form of religious worship was widely practiced in the home, it was much harder to control than public worship. Archeologists have uncovered plaster shrines and statues of protective household goddesses throughout the Mediterranean region, and even the areas occupied by the Israelites during this time (800 BCE). Female statues were housed in alcoves close to entrances, prayed to and anointed with oil. Incense burners used to purify and protect the house were often found in niches along with the figurines.[16] The Goddess was still the great protectress of women and children, but more quietly worshipped in the privacy of home. When food was prepared, she was given a libation in honor of her abundance. When children were born she was called to protect them. She was not forgotten, but instead became the personal household deity. Eventually, however, she was joined by male deities of the home, and in some cases replaced by them.

Classical Domestic Deities

During the classical era, in Egypt, Greece and Rome, household deities and guardians were very popular.

Isis was the most well-known goddess of the home, teacher of weaving, bread making, and medicine. She was worshipped for over 3,000 years as the Great Mother, in charge of moisture, the waters of life. She is often depicted wearing cow horns with a sun disk on her head.[17] She became a favorite deity of many people, both in Egypt and later in Rome where she was worshipped until the fourth century CE.

Taweret, portrayed as a female hippopotamus with pendulous breasts, was another popular goddess worshipped in Egyptian homes. She was the goddess of childbirth, an aspect of the great goddess Hathor. Another well-known Egyptian household deity was Bes, considered to be a foreign god, a rather strange-looking, bearded, dwarf-like character dressed in leopard skin and wearing an ostrich-feather headdress.[18]

The Grecian House Deity

The most widely honored Grecian house goddess was Hestia. She was the goddess of all domestic life and kept close watch over the hearth. From every meal cooked on the fire a portion was laid on the hearth and burned as a sacrifice to her. Although there were ancient circular temples dedicated to Hestia where a flame was kept continuously burning, she was more commonly worshipped privately than publicly.[19]

Deities of Roman Domiciles

Vesta, the Roman Goddess of the hearth, was the Latin equivalent of the Greek goddess Hestia. (A more ancient hearth goddess named Caca had a similar role in Etruscan culture.) Vesta was so popular that at one time it was said that in every Roman household there was a statue of her. The hearth was considered the center or heart of the home, and corresponded to the Roman's belief that the soul resided in the heart of the human body.[20]

Other popular Roman household deities were the *Penates,* who watched over the family cupboards, preserving the stores of food and wine. Their name was related to *penus,* the term for larder or pantry. They were closely allied with the family and were honored at the altar on the hearth alongside Vesta. It was customary to offer the Penates the first helping of food at each meal.

The *Lar*, an Etruscan word signifying chief or prince, performed the role of house guardian. He is depicted as a playful, dancing youth with curly hair, wearing a short tunic. There was only one family Lar who shared the hearth altar with the Penates and Vesta. During special celebrations these honored house deities were decorated with garlands of flowers and given libations of wine and fruit while incense was burned at their shrine. Lar literally became synonymous with the home—the term *ad larem suum reverti* meant to come home. The Lar was invoked on all important occasions of family life: births, marriages, and funerals. When a bride crossed the threshold of her new house she offered the Lar a sacrifice and gave him a coin for good luck.[21] A Pre-Roman festival, the *Larentalia,* honored the mother of the Lares, Acca Larentia (Lara), an Etruscan Goddess and the first Vestal Virgin.[22]

Each individual was imbued with a creative force called the *genius.* Honored on the day of birth and throughout the lifetime of the individual, the genius presided over marriage and the nuptial bed (the *genialis*).[23] Originally, the female counterpart was the Juno, or soul, of a woman. During the time of the Roman Empire, genius replaced Juno and came to mean the spirit of both male and female. Later, the term *genii loci* came to mean the spirit of place.[24]

Ancestors as Household Deities

In more ancient times the Lares were said to be artifacts (possibly skulls) that contained the spirits and wisdom of the dead ancestors. This practice can be traced back to the ancient civilization at Catalhoyuk, where skulls were found in temples, and what appears to be a venerated ancestor is buried without his head.[25] The practice of using the skulls of dead ancestors as totem and divinatory implements was also found in Celtic lore.[26] Even in the Bible, a story is told of ancient ancestral protective deities, the teraphim

that have also been identified as the skulls of the ancestors used as oracles.[27] Some of these skulls were
plastered and painted; the eye sockets filled in with
cowry shells, the ancient symbols of female genitals
used as universal protective amulets.[28]

Many early people kept the actual remains of their
ancestors with them. In Catalhoyuk, not only did they
use the skulls in their temples, their dead were kept
under the bed. Isn't it interesting that in much later
folklore we read of ghosts under the bed? And how
many of us as children intuitively sensed the presence
of spirits under our beds (ancient memories)?

The ancient Germanic people believed that the
souls of the dead had magical powers. This, and the
notion that souls stayed close to the body after death,
led to the custom of burying ancestors under the
threshold of the house to act as protective spirits. It
was also believed that innocent victims could be
avenged by these deceased ancestors, who might return to exact justice as they had appeared in human
form, or disguised as animals.[29]

Household Deities
in Ancient Europe

Before and after the expansion of the Roman Empire
into northern Europe, female deities were worshipped
in public and in the privacy of their homes as well.
These goddesses so reminiscent of the ancient god-

desses of the Mediterranean area were often depicted as a triune. (The triple aspect of the Goddess reflects the most ancient female symbol: the triangle.) Triads of mother goddesses, the *Deae Matres*, carrying children and cornucopia, with dogs at their feet, symbolized protection of children, abundant harvest, and healing. From earliest times, this trio of goddesses was found in almost all ancient mythological stories, often in the context of maiden, mother, and crone. The Romans' fates or fortunes, Juventas (virgin), Juno (mother), and Menarva or Minerva (wise crone), the Vikings' Norns; and the Greeks' Hebe, Hera, and Hecate all refer to this trinity.[30]

In Nordic mythology the triadic goddess Freya was associated with the household and was known for spinning yarn with her golden distaff and spindle. If a housewife was diligent in working her loom, it was believed that Freya might send down to her a piece of her own yarn, the yarn that could never be used up. Always seen with a set of keys hung from her belt, she was the protectress of marriages and childbirth. Freya and her two companion goddesses, Saga and Gefjon, were so much alike that the three were often seen as one. They were the goddesses that women prayed to for defense of their households during troubled times.[31]

Brigit, the mother goddess in the Celtic pantheon, is guardian of the household fire, much like Vesta and Hestia. Born at sunrise, giving the appearance that the house is bathed in fire, she was also invoked at night to protect the hearth while the household slept. Today, in the Outer Hebrides off the Scottish coast, she is still honored as the bride who is invited into the house during a special ceremony. Handmade images of her as the maiden are dressed in white and carried into the home in a basket while special songs and dances are performed.

More House Deities

In Lithuania, Aspelenie ruled the corner of the house behind the door, and Gabija, goddess of the hearth was honored by throwing salt into the flames. Malergabiae was a Fire goddess of the Lithuanian house, and the first loaf of bread was offered to her. Women used their fingers to indent the dough as a sign that the loaf was dedicated to her. Baba Yaga was a Slavic kitchen witch who lived in the last sheaf of grain, known to bring good fortune to the families she protected. A Celtic goddess of the horse and dog, Epona, was depicted with the cornucopia and the key which signified abundance and nurture. Haltia was the Baltic Finnish spirit who lived in the roof beams, kept an eye on the house, and stood guard over the family's wealth. Madder Akka, the Swedish goddess of birth and women's fertility, in one of her aspects as Uks Akka, the Old Lady of the Door, was present at births to receive the newborn baby. She lived beneath the threshold, blessing all those who left the home, much like the newborn leaving the womb. In Siberia, the hearth goddess was Poza-Mama, who kept the family warm. The first morsel of food was thrown into the fire in an offering to her. Rosmurta, the great provider and goddess of Fire, warmth, wealth, and abundance, was the flower queen of Gaul. She was opposed to marriage, and carried a two-headed axe, a cornucopia, basket of fruit, a stick with two snakes (caduceus), or a water bucket (all symbols of the ancient goddess). In Mexico the ancient goddess Tonantzin (Our Lady), was the mother goddess identified with the moon. Today, the Virgin of Guadalupe is still the household protectress venerated in shrines throughout the southwestern United States and Mexico.

1 Burleigh Muten, *Return of the Great Goddess*, New York: Stewart, Tabori and Chang, 1994, 1997.

2 Gimbutas, xx.

3 Ralph Metzner, *The Well of Remembrance*, Boston and London: Shambhala, 1994, 11.

4 Gadon, 24.

5 Macrone, 16.

6 Kris Waldherr, *The Book of Goddesses*, Hillsboro, OR: Beyond Words Publishing, 1995.

7 Walker, *Woman's Encyclopedia*, 339, 484.

8 Ibid, 324, 687.

9 Charlene Spretnak, *Lost Goddesses of Early Greece,* Boston: Beacon Press, 1978, 1992, 18.

10 Walker, *Woman's Encyclopedia*, 333.

11 Ibid, 125.

12 Walker, *Woman's Encyclopedia,* 908.

13 Muten, 52.

14 Victoria Ions, *Egyptian Mythology,* London: The Hamlyn Publishing Group Ltd., 1965, 1975, 63.

15 Ibid, 89, 91.

16 Elizabeth Ann Remington Willett, *Women and Household Shrines in Ancient Israel*, Ann Arbor, MI: University Microfilms,1999.

17 Waldherr.

18 Larousse, *Larousse Encyclopedia of Mythology*, New York: Barnes and Noble Books, 1994, 39.

19 Ibid, 136.

20 Ibid, 204.

21 Ibid, 218.

22 Walker, *Woman's Encyclopedia,* 16, 529.

23 Larousse, 217.

24 Walker, *Woman's Encyclopedia,* 339, 484.

25 Hoddard, Ion, Catalhoyuk Excavations,
    http://catal.arch.cam.ac.uk/catal/catal.html

26 Peter Berresford Ellis, *The Druids*, Grand Rapids, MI: William B. Eerdmans Publishing Co., 1994, 121.

27 Walker, *Woman's Encyclopedia,* 987.

28 Ibid, 182.

29 Larousse, 277.

30 Walker, *Woman's Encyclopedia,* 182, 1018.

31 Ingri D'Aulaire and Edgar Darin, *Norse Gods and Giants*, New York: Doubleday & Co., 1967.

Chapter 4

Deities or Demons?

From ghoulies and ghosties and long-leggedy
beasties and things that go bump in the night,
good Lord deliver me.[1]

Old Scottish prayer

Repression of Old Religions

For thousands of years the gods and goddesses commingled. During the Roman occupation of Europe, many Celtic and Norse gods and goddesses were incorporated into the pantheon of existing Roman deities. The Romans had a certain limited respect for the gods of the conquered peoples, often comparing them with their own. "In pre-Christian religion there was no obligation to accept a definite creed or even openly to acknowledge the power of the gods in one's own life. One could abandon a cult if one's luck failed."[2] However, as Christianity spread throughout the Roman Empire pantheism and goddess worship were suppressed by converted Roman

51

emperors—devout followers of the one God who could accept no other deities.

Loss of the Goddess

By the fifth century CE all temples of goddess worship were destroyed or converted into Christian churches. In about 300 CE Emperor Constantine brought an end to the ancient sanctuary of Ashtoreth at Aphaca, claiming it was immoral. In 380 CE Emperor Theodosius closed down the temple of the Goddess at Eleusis, and the seventh wonder of the world, the temple of the goddess Artemis (Diana) at Ephesus in western Anatolia. In 450 CE in Athens the Parthenon of the Acropolis was converted to a Christian church, and by the end of that century all remaining temples of Isis were closed.[3]

What once were considered sacred symbols and rites were deemed pagan signs and devil worship. Veneration of personal domestic deities was considered idolatry. Some of the rural areas and remote locations such as Iceland still retained a pantheistic theology of Celtic and Norse gods and goddesses until about 1000 CE, when the Scandinavian Vikings were Christianized.[4] Strongholds of Celtic belief during the Roman occupation, Wales, Ireland, and Scotland eventually merged some of their deities with the new religion; ancient gods and goddesses who would not die out became saints of the Catholic Church. The Celtic goddess Brigit (Brighid, Brigantia) became St. Brigid, the midwife of Mary, and foster mother of Jesus.

In most of Europe, Christianity became the only recognized religion. The early Christian God was a fierce
God whose wrath was feared; death was used as a
threat to those who refused obedience. People were led
to believe that they would die and disappear or burn
forever in a lake of fire and brimstone if they didn't
worship this particular deity. With the continuing
spread of the Christian church, most of the female
house deities were gradually disseminated. By the first
millennium, Mary, the mother of Jesus, was the only
female deity officially allowed in Europe, but whether
she was worshipped as Isis or Gaea (Gaia) or Mary, she
was the Mother of God, the Queen, and the Goddess.
Her name never had been important, but often reflected aspects of her divine nature: vulture, cave, womb,
serpent, all names for the Mother Goddess.

Worship of female deities went underground during
the Dark Ages. Arcane symbols such as the archway
(Omega) or stylized flowers like roses, lilies, and fleur
de lis (Western varieties of the lotus blossom, a well-
known Eastern yonic symbol) or fruits with multiple
seeds, like pomegranates and figs (all long associated
with the life-producing anatomy of the Divine Feminine), became a covert language and were inserted in
religious paintings and artifacts. Although one was told
what to believe in church, the sacred Feminine was still
worshipped by the common people in their homes.
Shrines were kept and rituals performed in her honor.
In many cultures bread was baked in identifying shapes,

such as croissants in the shape of the crescent moon, or special decorations were placed on top of the bread before it was baked to signify that it was a special offering to the Goddess. Salt was believed to be symbolic of her blood, and was deemed unlucky if spilled. More than ever it became necessary to worship the ancient Goddess in the privacy of the home, where she was honored and treated as a personal protectress and healer. Her name varied, but the symbolism was the same.

Eventually all female deities, with the exception of Mary and a few others, who became Christian saints, were turned into hags, witches, and demons. Their sacred symbols became known as tools of the devil. Elves and fairies took the place of the ancient Goddess of the Home, and Mary was worshipped as the "Queen of Heaven," removing her from the more mundane issues in the earthly realm. Domestic spirits took on a mischievous and sometimes sinister character; their appearance ranged from humorous to frightening.

Since Celtic worship was often outside in nature near streams, in sacred groves, or in private homes, it was more difficult to eradicate. The legend of Merlin retained vestiges of druidic forest magic for centuries, although he became more Christianized over time. Throughout Europe, pockets of rural "simple folk" maintained belief in house spirits, referring to them as elves, fairies, and gnomes. Some of these "little people," such as the *brownies* of Scotland, bore a marked resemblance to the brown-cloaked Druids of earlier

Celtic nature worship. The widespread belief in fairies has been explained as memories of an earlier culture displaced by more powerful invaders.[5]

Teutonic and Norse Household Deities

In Teutonic mythology, elves installed themselves in people's houses and became familiar spirits known as *kobolds*. The kobolds were seen as little old men with wrinkles and pointed hoods. They made themselves useful by doing household chores and bringing good luck to the households who sheltered them. They demanded a small price for their services, some milk and leftovers; but if they were forgotten, they could be vindictive. It was thought that a broken dish or burned pot was the act of a scorned kobold.[6] Elves were originally the spirits of the dead ancestors who brought fertility.

Slavonic Mythology

The name for the Russian house spirits, the *Domovoi*, was derived from the word *dom*, meaning house. Although their appearance was similar to humans, they were covered with a sort of silky fur and sometimes depicted with horns and a tail (probably a leftover from the demonized female house spirit). When a new house was built, the wife would put a slice of bread under the stove to attract a Domovoi to her new home. He would live either near the stove or under the threshold to protect the front door. The wife of the Domovoi, called *Domania* or *Domovikha*, made her home in the cellar (a sure sign of her demoted status). It was her job to protect the home and to warn the inhabitants of any trouble that might threaten them.

In some regions *Kikimora*, a domestic spirit, was known as Domovoi's wife. She took part in all household tasks and was especially helpful if the woman of the house was industrious. If she was lazy, Kikimora would cause mischief and tickle the children during the night. In order to regain her favor, the housewife had to gather ferns from the forest and prepare a fern tea. She was then required to wash all the pots and pans in the house with this special tea. Kikimora is portrayed in a 1934 drawing by I. Bilibin as a long-snouted, chicken-footed, horned peasant woman with furry ears, wearing a scarf over her long, stringy hair.[7]

Celtic House Spirits

A similar character in Scottish folklore, the brownie was a popular spirit who, if treated well, would help with the drudgery of the housework while the occupants slept. Brownies were generally regarded as hairy beings with no nose and only small nostrils in their flat little faces. Their good nature made up for their rather odd appearance. In the British Isles, elves, pixies, and fairies proliferate, and their reference to earlier Druidic nature spirits is a generally accepted belief. Hobgoblins originally were house spirits (*hob* relates to hearth), but later myths portray them as fearsome creatures that with other more sinister gremlins haunt the home.

Universal Belief in Household Spirits

Household spirits were found in all parts of the world, and although they were known under various names they all had a similar function: to provide food and protection for the family shelter. In Spain one would have found the *duende*, in France *esprit follet*, in America the guardian angel, in Scandinavia the *nis* or *nisse*, and throughout Europe bogies, fairies, pixies, puck, Robin Goodfellow, sprites, sylphs, trolls, and the White Lady of Ireland to name a few.

Renaissance and Age of Enlightenment

The Renaissance era brought a revival of classical mythology; symbols of Greek and Roman gods and goddesses reappeared in fashionable paintings. During the witch hunts of the Age of Enlightenment, almost all symbols associated with the ancient Mother and the Old European earth-based religions were labeled as diabolic. A Machiavellian tactic is to project the nature of the true enemy onto the one who has been vanquished; also known as "demonizing the enemy." It is very sobering to look at the sacred symbols of Mother

Earth and see the evil connotations given them during the past 2,000 years.

Sacred or Evil?

The fruits of the sacred trees were already associated with Eve's offering of the apple to Adam as the fatal act of temptation that brought expulsion from the Garden of Eden, pain of childbirth, the brand of "harlot" on woman's sexuality, and the awful fact that all newborn babies were born in sin (from the sinful act of coitus). The fig and the pomegranate, symbolic of female genitals and fertility, were considered worthless fruits (too full of seeds). The sacred wisdom and immortality of the snake became the temptations of the devil himself. "According to ancient British custom, simply coming across an adder is bad luck, unless the snake is killed immediately."[8]

The vulture was a flesh-eating harbinger of death. Birds of the night (the time of the moon), bats, and owls became the dastardly companions of witches. At one time owls were considered wise, the sacred companion of Athena, but during the shameful time of the Inquisition, the owl lost its good standing and became instead an evil accomplice.

Cats were long associated with the Norse goddess Freya and the Egyptian goddess Bast. They pulled Freya's wagon across the sky, rode in chariots with their owners in Egypt, and were buried in sacred tombs. In ancient Egypt it was considered a crime to kill a cat; some say it carried the death penalty. After the northern European countries were converted to Christianity, Freya was consigned to the mountains as a witch, Friday (named after her) became the day chosen by witches for their meetings, and the cat became known as the witch's steed.[9] Cats were held in such disdain in medieval Europe they were killed on sight. Some historians believe the bubonic plague occurred because of the huge rat population arising from the extermination of their natural predator, the cat.

It was considered bad luck to sleep in moonlight; one could become moonstruck, or even worse, a lunatic (crazed by the moon—luna). Women's menstrual cycles were evil and taboo—to even look at a menstruating woman was considered bad luck. If a menstruating woman so much as touched a beehive all the bees would fly away and never return.[10]

Once revered as divine procreators of the human race, women were now considered sexual temptresses and men their unwilling prey. Abstinence was encouraged as the more righteous path to heaven. If one did marry, then sex was a necessary evil, but only for procreative purposes, never for pleasure. Pregnant women often stayed indoors, their swollen conditions a clear indication of their participation in the wanton sex act. Nursing was even deemed unladylike and wet nurses were employed to perform this crass deed. All parts of a woman's body were considered shameful.

Sacred vs Superstition

One of the objections we should address is: if we adopt some of these ancient symbols and rituals concerning our personal dwellings, will we also adopt fearful, ignorant superstitions and misleading assumptions? This is a question that has bothered many contemporary spiritual seekers who desire some sort of ritual or sacred practice as a part of their lives, but do not want to revert to dangerous, ill-formed notions or plain hocus-pocus. They have a healthy aversion to our predecessor's unwarranted fears of witches and the "Evil Eye" that caused many innocent people to lose their lives. What then separates the two?

From the overwhelming historical and archeological evidence we learn that our ancient ancestors had an immanent relationship to their deity. In the earliest religion, God was not a punitive father figure somewhere up in the sky just waiting to catch them sinning so he could pronounce judgment, but instead she was present among them birthing new life, nourishing in unique and creative ways, and recycling all matter so that not a cell was wasted.

It is my firm belief that a sacred reverence for the natural order and cycles of life with the knowledge that life is never destroyed, but regenerated, is a doctrine that alleviates the fear of death. This doctrine, rather than supporting fears of the unknown that give rise to superstitions, frees the mind to observe, explore, and venerate the beauty and sacredness of all life forms. There is a simple test to judge whether you are falling prey to superstitious beliefs or sacred knowledge—fear. If the dogma you are considering is shrouded in fear, then you are looking at superstition. If, on the other hand, you adopt symbols and rituals that instill acceptance and reverence toward all life and all beings, you are embracing sacred principles. For example, when we can see the vulture as nature's way of recycling dead flesh, rather than as an evil harbinger of death, we see the miraculous cycle of life. Likewise, to eliminate our phobia of reptiles, due to their supposed association with Satan, sin, the curse of women, and the downfall of men, is a wonderfully freeing decision. When we respect another's space we are watchful when walking in the desert or forest where we might encounter snakes and other potentially harmful animals, rather than arming ourselves with weapons to mindlessly exterminate them.

There is a marvelous loving attitude that comes with reverence for the Earth Mother and all of her creations. It also carries with it a respect for so-called inanimate aspects of nature. The earth itself is a living entity much like our bodies, and we in turn are like the cells of the earth. When we poison our environment with careless toxins dumped into the air and waterways or denude the forests of trees or the mountains of minerals, we are damaging our own bodies. How can we not be aware that the air we breathe, the water we drink, the plants and animals that we eat are as much a part of our bodies as our fingers and toes? How can we keep on poisoning our larger body and expect to keep our "personal" body alive? The belief in the sacred nature of the universe is to free ourselves of limiting superstitions and to fully become one with all that is.

Throughout history, fear has been used to control the masses and to eliminate a belief in one's personal power and the ability to have a one-on-one relationship with one's own deity. When a warring dominant force overcomes a more peaceful community, the conquerors historically impose their beliefs and religion upon the "ignorant heathens" of the conquered nation. The next step is to eradicate any residual belief in the old religions. Dominating and then keeping people subservient has been the course of history for the last several thousand years. We are now witnessing the final stage of this domination where even the most remote pockets of habitation that retained a tiny vestige of their primitive beliefs have been ferreted out and destroyed. There is no one "bad guy" here. Every major civilization in modern history has repeated this pattern, but there is a wonderful light in this tunnel. We now know that this is not the nature of all humankind, and that, for the greater part of history, peaceful societies existed without weapons of war.[11,12,13]

Spirituality Left Home

Most Celtic and European religions, prior to the Roman occupation, were not formally practiced in churches but were nature centered; based on the belief that spirit was manifest in all things. When spiritual practices were taken out of the home, they became institutionalized and controlled. People were no longer in charge of their own spirituality, but instead were directed to professional middlemen who would convey their message and let them know what was expected in return. As we incorporate sacred objects and reintroduce ancient rituals into our homes, we bring spirituality into our everyday lives. We decide how and when and in what way we will honor our own personal deity.

The spirits of the home (the ancient ancestors) are personal deities who have been venerated since the beginning of time. There are no rules or dogma associated with honoring the spirits of place, the genii loci. Each person decides for her- or himself the most meaningful way to offer gratitude for each day's gifts.

Balancing Male and Female Energy

Because we have just ended the second millennium, a time when dominant patriarchal monotheistic religions reigned almost universally, with the nearly complete annihilation of feminine deities, the obvious reaction is to advocate a return to a matrifocal or even matriarchal society. Hopefully we can learn from history so we are not doomed to repeat it. In design one of the most basic principles is balance. Today, many people engaged in spiritual practice are committed to balancing male and female energies. To simply advocate swinging the pendulum from the oppressive male patriarchal dogmatic religions back to a matriarchal or feminine-centered belief system is missing the obvious lesson.

In balancing energies, the shadow side seeks equilibrium with the light side. Quiet walks in pristine forests with the sounds of birds chirping may seem idyllic, but there are other natural occurrences. Fires and floods are not all manmade. The earth is cyclical, continually destroying and regenerating. Lightning strikes and thunder rolls. Much like a forest fire and the regeneration of pine trees that spread their seeds after fire, the natural cycle of things includes purification, death, and regeneration.

It is not possible to eliminate aggression by deeming it hateful and imprisoning it. We must seek to acknowledge and incorporate our own aggression—not disown it, or euphemize only the cooperative and placid. We must find the common basis for respect of all human beings, all animals, and all matter. We must reincorporate the sacred in every aspect of our lives and our thinking. Bringing spirituality back into our homes is a step in the right direction for regaining personal power and thus balancing the scale between rigid dogma and intuitive personal belief.

1 www.Beliefnet.com.

2 H. R. Ellis Davidson, *Myths and Symbols in Pagan Europe,* Syracuse, NY: Syracuse University Press, 1988, 223.

3 Stone, *When God Was a Woman,* Orlando, FL: Harcourt Brace and Co., 1976, 18.

4 Davidson, 2.

5 Ibid, 112.

6 Larousse, 279.

7 Ibid, 289.

8 David Pickering, *Cassell Dictionary of Superstitions,* London: Cassell Wellington House, 1995, 3.

9 De Lys, 97–98.

10 Ibid, 46.

11 Gimbutas, xx.

12 Gadon, 24.

13 Metzner, 35.

Chapter 5

Protecting the Sacred Home

The threshold was sacred because beyond it lay
the sacred hearth and the dwelling of the house
spirit.[1]

G. L. Gomme, 1883

Drawing the Sacred Circle

Ancient temples often had walkways around the
perimeter of the structure called ambulatories (they are
also found in gothic and medieval churches.) This ceremony of creating a circle for protection recreates the
earliest symbol for the belly of the Great Mother. To
walk the perimeter three times counterclockwise, while
chanting a prayer or calling on the spirits of place, was
the most ancient way of protecting a building or property. (During the Dark Ages, counterclockwise [widder-
shins] was considered the witch's direction and the
custom of ambulating a property was changed to the

clockwise direction). The left has always been the feminine side or direction, and also the reason the left side was later considered bad luck. It wasn't just a simple notion of getting out on the right side of the bed, putting the right foot forward, or using the right hand for shaking hands or taking an oath—we were told that it was terribly unlucky to do otherwise.[2]

The spiritual home started at its boundaries, and those boundaries were deemed sacred in many ancient customs.

The Sacred Threshold

Since ancient times the threshold was believed to be the entrance (vulva) into the body (womb) of the Goddess. When you stepped across the threshold, it was considered a sacred act. You were entering a holy place! And since the threshold marked the primary entrance to the home, it was also the most vulnerable place for undesirable influences to enter.

Our earliest example of a sacred threshold symbol is the Goddess of Laussel herself, and the triangular shape that represents the entrance to her sacred womb. It's rather curious to look at the average doorway and see symbols of the female anatomy that are naturally present. Some say the triangle with the apex at the bottom is associated with the feminine anatomy, whereas the triangle with the apex at the top is symbolic of male principles, but triangles were known from ancient times as the female trinity, monogram of the Goddess, and the Delta, the holy door—the vulva [fig. 11].[3]

Figure 11

Basic architecture and interior design courses teach that the triangular shape over the doorway in many homes (the pediment) originated with the Greeks. The ancient tombs of Mycenea circa 1500 BCE clearly incorporated pediments (huge triangular recesses carved from megalithic stones) over the entrance openings. This classical architectural device of the pediment over the doorway has become a common feature in American homes. In the early nineteenth century Greek Revival became a popular style of architecture in America. One of the main features of this style is the triangular gable that faces the street, analogous to ancient temple pediments. Other housing styles continued to use this feature throughout the nineteenth and twentieth centuries, making it a prevalent element of the American home. Thus, unintentionally, American architects and home builders have generously incorporated a sacred symbol into many of our homes.

The archway in Spanish and Moorish architecture is the yonic symbol. Omega, the great OM, is the horseshoe shape. Alpha and Omega, the beginning and the end, both refer to the Mother's womb [fig. 12].[4] Many homes in the Southwest of the United States have an arched entryway

Figure 12

typical of Mediterranean-style architecture—again thanks to the unknowing architects who have continued to use this revered shape.

Two vertical stone or wooden columns, with a header (lintel) extending horizontally over the top just

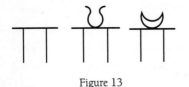

Figure 13

beyond the pillars, found among many sacred rock formations such as Stonehenge, is an ancient symbol of the altar and hearth. This same symbol with horn-like protrusions on the top is also the sign of Hestia and Vesta, the ancient Greek and Roman house deities.[5] The symbol is said to represent her hearth and fire. Horns in the shape of the crescent moon over the entrance have been symbolic of sacred space since the early Neolithic era [fig. 13].

Look at your own entryway. What is the shape of the door? Is there a triangular pediment over the door? Is your entryway arched? If there are no obvious references to the sacred nature of the space you are about to enter, consider using a symbol from the following suggestions, or one of your own, to remind yourself that as you enter this home, you are entering holy ground.

Threshold Amulets

The Horseshoe

Since the threshold was the most vulnerable area, many objects and symbols have been used there as protective icons. Traditionally, these amulets were used as symbolic prayers and petitions to the Great Mother or to ancestors to protect the home from negative or destructive forces. These icons are also simple reminders of the reverence we need to have for our homes. They remind us that any anger or irreverence that we bring home is left outside as we enter our sacred dwellings with peace. In many cultures shoes were left outside, not just because of the mud or dirt they brought in, but also because of the negative energy with which they had come in contact.

A well-known threshold amulet, the horseshoe is the classic shape of Omega, the symbol of the Goddess's Great Gate. Superstitions say that to place the horseshoe with the opening facing down is to lose all of the luck contained in it, so it was often reversed. As we have explained earlier, most of the symbols of female anatomy were disguised or reversed in medieval Europe, and their traditional meanings were eventually lost. If used as a protective amulet, the horseshoe is hung with the opening facing down, as in the archway or Omega [fig. 14].

Figure 14

Have you ever wondered about the deeper significance of a horseshoe over a doorway? Have you used one yourself without realizing the ancient significance?

Ancestors and Protective Deities

The actual remains of the ancestors were often buried under the entrance of the home to protect the inhabitants. Spirits of deceased ancestors were considered household guardians, and their bones, or objects symbolizing them, were placed near the entrance to the home. The Celts revered the skulls of ancestors and used them in their homes to bring in good luck. Since the head was considered the area of the body that held consciousness and wisdom, skulls were also consulted for divination purposes. This is probably why many Greek and Roman households had a bust of a god, goddess, or powerful ruler in their home. From the most ancient times onward we find the spirits of ancestors being called upon to protect the living, especially in vulnerable areas of the home.

From the Roman's vast pantheon of gods and goddesses several specific ones were assigned to guard the front door. Janus (Ianus) was the god of doors, gates, and beginnings. He had two faces, one looking forward and one looking backward, watching both directions at once. The threshold was also guarded by the god Limentinum and the goddess Lima. Cardea was goddess of door hinges and Carna the goddess of door handles. Forculus was the god of the door and Portunus the protector of the door.[5] It seems much more romantic than the array of locks and bolts on present-day doors, but nevertheless illustrates the importance of protecting the main entrance to the home.

Other Threshold Amulets

Crosses were the most prevalent threshold icons throughout the Middle Ages and even today in Christian homes. The obvious association is with the crucifixion of Jesus and with his power to ward off evil influences. It was believed that a cross of straw or sticks laid on the ground would trip a witch; and when placed above the door could prevent the entrance of witches,[6] stemming from the belief that if you trip when crossing the threshold you either bring bad luck to the home, or are yourself a witch.[7] Wives were first carried over the threshold to prevent them from tripping and bringing bad luck to the home.

The cross is an ancient symbol representing the four directions or four corners of the earth. Early crosses often had directional right angles (sauvastika) indicating the direction of the sun's movements (clockwise; masculine), others had counterclockwise right angles (sauvastika) representing the moon (feminine).[8] Brigid's crosses (counterclockwise swastikas) are ancient fertility symbols used to protect the harvest and farm animals [fig. 15].

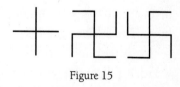

Figure 15

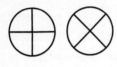

Figure 16

The equal-armed cross enclosed in a circle represents the four corners of the earth (a female symbol) also a solar disc or chariot wheel (a male symbol). This symbol is balanced in both male and female energy [fig. 16].

The Tau cross (T) is said to have far greater phallic significance than the equal-armed cross. Ancient inscriptions of the Tau cross have even been found with penis and testicles depicted on them. It is also associated with the sword, a powerful male symbol. The hammer of Thor and the axe are similar male power symbols, also associated with the power of iron as a prophylactic charm. The Tau cross under the loop in the Egyptian ankh is thought to represent the male principle, while the loop represents the female principle, making this another example of a balanced male/ female symbol. The ankh signifies eternal life.

As a wooden cross, there are many ancient associations. Wood was long considered a sacred material (knock on wood for good luck). The Druids used two crossed limbs from the sacred oak tree as a symbol of their God. The traditional Christian wooden cross has ancient associations with the tree of life, worshipped in many cultures as the original birthplace of mankind. The ancient goddess Asherah's statue was often sculpted with her lower body (trunk) representing a wooden pillar; she was worshipped in sacred groves.

Merlin lived in the forest in an apple tree, Odin hung from the sacred Yggdrasill tree for nine days; shamans the world over believe the roots of the world tree (*axis mundi*), growing deep into the earth with its branches reaching high into the heavens, connects the lower and upper worlds [fig. 17].

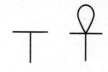

Figure 17

The Pentagram

The pentagram (five-pointed star is older than written characters, and was a magic charm for the Babylonians. Used throughout history as a defensive icon protecting the entrance to the home from demons; it was known as the emblem of happy homecoming.[9] An ancient symbol of the goddess Kore (Ceres), the pentagram is observable in the seeds and flesh of the apple's core when it is cut horizontally. Greeks considered the pentagram perfect geometry, the Druids viewed it as a sign of the Godhead, and the Hebrews as Solomon's seal. Again, as with many other symbols, it became associated with Satan during the Dark Ages, especially in its reversed aspect—known as the goblins' cross [fig. 18].

Figure 18

Hex Signs

Among the Old World customs that German immigrants to the United States brought with them was the use of prophylactic charms painted over the entrance to homes and barns. These colorful Hex signs were found throughout the countryside of Pennsylvania where a sizable population of Swiss and German immigrants settled in the 1700s and 1800s. Commonly referred to as the Pennsylvania Dutch, the original word was *Deutch* (German).[10] Most current information regarding Hex signs downplays the roles of these symbols as protective talismans, but the actual symbols reveal ancient meanings. Common symbols found on Hex signs are pentagrams, stars, crescent moons, birds, three-petal flowers, roses, pomegranates, oak leaves, solar wheels, swastikas, and hearts. An earlier use of Hex signs was to protect the home and barn animals from *heverei* (witchcraft).

A protective threshold guardian can be any symbol, plaque, or statue that represents the opening to the sacred womb, or other protective power symbol. You may choose to honor an ancestral deity here by burying a small piece of jewelry or artifact that belonged to a beloved ancestor in a potted plant by the front door, or perhaps a more visible reminder will help you remember that you are entering sacred ground. It can be stylized so only you know the meaning (triangle, wavy line, circle with a dot in the middle), or more well known, like a horseshoe, or horns. It might be fun to paint or stencil a design over the entry door like a three-petal flower, a bird, pentagram, or crescent moon; the choice is yours and the choices are limitless.

For example, I hung a delightful wooden folk-art figure of the head and wings of a Mexican angel over the door of my home in the Southwest; she makes a charming threshold protectress. In my cabin in the Northwest, I have an old horseshoe over the front door and a set of horns over the back door. If you prefer something less obtrusive, a small medal or lucky coin can be laid on top of the door frame. Whether proudly displayed or hidden, the point is to find something that feels right for you and represents your own aesthetic tastes and spiritual beliefs.

Can you think of something symbolic that you would like to use as a protective amulet or reminder of the sacredness of your home?

The Entryway

Just inside the threshold is the entryway into the home. In Roman households, the first thing seen when entering the home was the *Lararium* or household shrine, a small shrine or niche containing the statues or objects of familial protection, where the *lar* or household guardian was kept. In ancient European belief, a huge woman related to the Valkyries or the Disir called the Hamingja was the guardian spirit of the family. She was able to pass luck to the family members and provide them with special powers. The ruling gods were one class of divinity, but there was a deep-seated belief in separate and individual supernatural protectors and guardians.[11] Whether it's a Lar or

Hamingja, the entryway is an ideal place for a familial deity.

In our entryways we often have a table to hold our keys or handbag. Why not add some wonderful artifacts here and create a household shrine. If it's important for you to have a more private shrine, a beautiful small box with tiny amulets inside works well. In my current home, the first thing you see when entering is an antique wicker table with a large Spanish bowl on top filled with dried pomegranates, apples, and nuts (all symbolic of the abundance of Mother Earth). On the shelf underneath I display a beautiful Huichol (Mexican Indian) beaded snake, an ancient symbolic house guardian. Use your imagination and you will come up with something personally meaningful.

The Hearth

The hearth is considered the heart of the home, the altar and the navel of the Mother's womb. It is also a commentary of our times that many homes no longer have a hearth, replaced instead with a television. Fire was considered sacred energy to our forebears, with deities specifically named as goddess of the hearth; Brigit, Hestia, Vesta, and a score of others stood guard over this holy element in the home. Altars were placed here for thousands of years, and food or salt was thrown into the fire or burned on the hearth as an offering and sign of appreciation to these protective deities. The symbol of the snake, an ancient protective household icon, is associated with the life energy symbolic of the fire in the hearth.

Aside from the door, the chimney was another vulnerable entrance that needed protection. Amulets of all kinds have traditionally been used on the fireplace to protect the home from invasive spirits.

Bedrooms

As our ancestors lay down to sleep and dream, their defenses were also down. Sleeping areas were susceptible to harmful intruders and undesirable energies or spirits. As previously discussed, it was a widely held notion that the dead could protect the living. In the ancient civilization of Catalhoyuk, we learned of the practice of burying the dead under the sleeping platforms. Celtic lore tells of sleeping on the fairy mounds (burial mounds) for inspiration. In Greece, dreams were an important part of healing and divination. Shamanic practitioners use an altered state of sleep for their work. The shaman must be protected during this time and his/her sleep uninterrupted. In Egypt, protective deities were carved or placed on the bedposts. Throughout history, fertility symbols were commonly found in bedrooms. Water animals such as fish, frogs, snakes, and birds (the stork is a remnant of the custom of using water birds as symbols of childbirth and fertility) and water flowers such as lotus and water lilies were used as fertility symbols, as were fruits containing seeds and nuts.

Your bedroom is the ideal place for treasured family photographs. A keepsake such as your grandmother's locket placed on your dresser, or figures of water birds, fish, frogs, or flowers on your bedside table are ways to bring sacred symbols into your dream space. What sacred artifacts would you like to display in your own bedroom?

Protection from the Evil Eye

The Evil Eye is perhaps the most feared omen, accompanied by more protective devices than any other in all mythology. There is general disagreement as to the origin of the term, but its roots are ancient. In early Minoan cultures the snake was a symbol of wisdom and resurrection. Snake goddesses were revered for healing and prophecy. The wisdom of the snake goddess and the symbol of the snake became synonymous. In ancient Egypt the snake was used as a headdress, the *uraeus*, worn by gods and pharaohs. The snake's eyes were positioned over the middle of the forehead in the area known as the third eye, the place of intuitive or prophetic vision. The all-seeing-eye was once associated with Maat, the Egyptian goddess of truth and judgment.[12] Later, the snake represented the guardian of the home and the infallible conqueror of the Evil Eye.[13]

This eye of wisdom, or All-Seeing Eye, is the subject of numerous legends in many cultures, and, as we have already discussed, what was once considered sacred was later profane. Both the Egyptian sun god Ra and Horus had one searing eye. The Norse god Odin had only one eye, as his other eye was given in exchange for wisdom. In Roman mythology, the eye of Medusa, whose hair was snake-ridden, was said to strike terror and death with a penetrating stare. Thus the All-Seeing Eye came to mean the Evil Eye; the ability of a person with magical powers to cast a spell or lay a curse with a look. During the Inquisition, accused witches were made to enter the court backward so they wouldn't be allowed the first eye contact.[14] Fear of the Evil Eye has borne such expressions as "if looks could kill," and "her eyes were shooting daggers at me." Saliva was the supreme antidote for the Evil Eye.[15] Thus, to spit at someone was considered a major insult, accusing them of evil intentions.

Blue and green "eye" beads are still worn in many third world countries as protection from the Evil Eye. The principle of using an eye to avert an eye is the concept of reflecting back the bad luck to the originator. Hand signals are also widely used prophylactic charms to avert the Evil Eye. The *mano fico,* or fig hand, is a gesture of putting the thumb between the bent index and middle fingers. This symbol originally represented the female vulva, and like all genital areas was revered as sacred. Cowrie shells also represented female genitals and are widely used on fetishes as protective charms. The most prolifically used protective charms throughout history are symbols of female reproductive parts and male genitals.

The so-called "Evil Eye" was once the "All-Seeing-Eye," a symbol of prophesy or truth. We can all use the power to detect when someone is not being truthful. Can you identify this symbol on any of your household arti-facts? Small eye beads can be purchased at stores where beads and supplies are sold. Put one in your small shrine box to see clearly and know the truth.

---

1 G. L. Gomme, *Folklore Relics of Early Village Life,* London, Elliot Stock, 1883.

2 Pickering, 26.

3 Walker, *Women's Encyclopedia,* 1016.

4 Ibid., 414.

5 Rudolf Koch, *The Book of Signs*, New York: Dover Publications, Inc., 1955, 53.

6 Larousse.

7 Pickering, 75.

8 De Lys, 183.

9 Walker, *Woman's Dictionary*, 61.

10 Koch, 6.

11 Edred Thorsson, *Northern Magic,* St. Paul, MN: Llewellyn World-wide Ltd., 1993, 137.

12 Davidson, 222, 122.

13 Walker, *Women's Encyclopedia*, 1028.

14 De Lys, 94.

15 Walker, *Women's Encyclopedia*, 294.

16 De Lys, 157.

PART TWO

Creating Sacred Homes

Chapter 6

Essential Elements

Indo-European tradition said the four elements were created by Great Mother Kali, who organized them into letter-mantras carved on her rosary of skulls, to form the Sanskrit alphabet... [1]

Barbara Walker

Basic Elements

On every continent in the world ancient symbols representing four cardinal points have been found. From the Aztecs to the Egyptians, the Tibetans to the Zunis, the four cardinal directions (and in many cultures the four elements) are represented by timeless symbols dating from as far back as Neolithic rock art. In Western culture, although the four directions and four elements were associated with the ancient Orphic mysteries, the idea of four basic elements has been historically credited to Empedocles, a fifth-century BCE

Greek healer and philosopher.[2] By the time of Aristotle, it was generally agreed by Greek metaphysicians and scientists that four basic elements made up all matter: solid matter (Earth), liquid (Water), gas (Air), and combustible energy (Fire). They also acknowledged a fifth element they called Quintessence, derived from the Latin words *quinta* (fifth) and *esse* (to be). This referred to Ether or Spirit. According to the ancient Greeks, the four elements plus Spirit make up the entire cosmos. All creativity was the result of manipulation of the four elements in ratios that would produce harmonious results. The fifth essence was the governing element (or life force) permeating all vital creation.

Directions and Seasons

Each element was assigned a cardinal direction and a season. In most instances, the pairing of elements with seasons and compass directions was based on the sun's yearly cycle. Seasons related to the position of the sun during the two solstices (winter and summer) and the two equinoxes (spring and autumn). When assigning elements to these cardinal points, we find many discrepancies, due in part to geographical and weather differences. For instance, the scorching summer sun of Egypt that dried up the welcome waters of the Nile and created drought conditions was not viewed in the same benevolent manner as it was in northern Europe where its coveted warmth was necessary to prevent frost during the short growing season. Therefore, the summer season symbolized the heat of Fire to the Egyptians and inhabitants of other Mediterranean countries, but represented a fertile period of Earth to northern Europeans. To some, the sun was a most welcomed visitor, to others it was a destructive force. Winter air was the same. In the southern Mediterranean climate, winter air was moist and warm, bringing tropical storms, whereas in northern regions it was cold and dry. The Greeks applied the elements according to their world view, from the standpoint of local geography and climate.

Calendars also varied. A calendar based on moon cycles had a larger range of weather patterns from one year to the next for the same seasons because of the shifting dates needed to make up for the fewer calendar days.

In fact, there are as many different assignments of elements to seasons as there are possibilities. After studying several different cultural patterns, and the relations of the elements to the seasons, we chose to adopt those associations based on northern climate conditions typical of Europe and North America. We also took into account information gleaned from folktales and myths relating to archetypal personages associated with each element, early goddess moon-based calendars, the primary and nearly universal belief in the primordial waters of life as the original birthplace, and the triple aspect of the ancient Mother: maiden, mother, crone (and death). The maiden (Persephone) represents springtime, when she returned to earth and was born like Venus from the waters of life. In summer the mother aspect is exemplified by Mother Nature's abundant produce symbolized by the earth goddess' (Demeter, Gaea, and Hera) horn of plenty; in autumn the crone (Hecate) is associated with Fire, the setting sun, the burning of stalks and rubble, the end of harvest, and the end of her reproductive life. Perhaps she is burned away in the Fires and carried high into the cold, barren winter sky (Air) where she is seemingly gone, only to be born again from the rain in the spring.

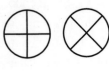

Figure 19

Symbolically pictured by the equal-armed cross inside a circle, the cycle of life continues to revolve: spring, summer, autumn, winter; maiden, mother, crone, death [fig. 19].

When we merge earth-based feminine archetypes with male sky gods and shamans we create a unique archetypal model merging aspects of both male and female energies and characteristics. (See chapter 7, Archetypal Design Styles.)

The Elements and Other Associations

In astrology, the four elements are associated with the signs of the Zodiac: Pisces, Cancer, and Scorpio with Water; Taurus, Virgo, and Capricorn with Earth; Aries,

Leo, and Sagittarius with Fire; and Aquarius, Gemini, and Libra with Air.

In the Tarot, the four elements are associated with the four suits: cups—Water (emotion/love); pentacles—Earth (physical/wealth); swords—Air (mental/justice); and wands—Fire (psychic/spiritual). In decks of common playing cards, hearts are related to cups (Water); diamonds to pentacles (Earth); clubs to wands (Fire); and spades to swords (Air).

The Four Temperaments

According to Jungian psychology there are four basic temperaments that account for the way people relate to the world around them: thinking, feeling, sensing, and intuition. When we assign these temperaments to the characteristics of the elements, we find that *thinking* is related to the mental element Air, *feeling* relates to the emotional element Water, *sensing* to the physical element Earth, and *intuition* to the creative element Fire. According to Jung, each person can identify with one of these temperaments as a dominant trait. If you are a thinking type you use your mind to figure out logically what it is you need to know to successfully function. An emotional Water type relies on feelings to relate to his surroundings. An Earth person is grounded in the five senses and understands the world according to what she sees, hears, smells, tastes, and touches. Those who relate closely to Fire are highly intuitive and creative, usually acting on hunches and gut feelings.

Let's take, for example, the purchase of a new home. Each temperament will use a different method to retrieve information and make a decision.

A thinking (Air) type will use his mind to figure out taxes and insurance, how much he can afford to pay for the house and still budget for all the other household expenses. He considers how the surrounding neighborhood will affect the market value, how his existing furniture will work and what he will need to purchase to furnish the house. This type probably deems it a weakness to let emotions sway him, and as for smells and noises—he's usually so busy thinking he doesn't notice. Dominant Air people are very skeptical of acting on hunches.

A feeling (Water) type will rely on her emotions about the house. Typical phrases that this personality type might use when determining whether or not to buy a particular house would be: "I felt so loved and protected when I walked in the door. It was as if I were coming home," "I absolutely love this house. I don't care if we need to stretch the budget," or "I don't know what it is, but there is a really yucky feeling in this house."

A sensing (Earth) person will probably run his fingers over surfaces, and crawl under the sink to look for drips. Sensing people want a functional kitchen and possibly a space for a garden. They might walk through a house and touch the materials, closely look-ing at the workmanship, or be quickly turned off by offensive smells or the noise of a highway near by.

An intuitive (Fire) person will act on a hunch. "I'm not sure what it was about the house, but everything said, 'Buy it!'" "I had a strong hunch this was the right house for me."

The elemental temperaments are incomplete without interaction. The mental giant spends all his time con-templating the nature of the universe and forgets to feel the sun on his back or smell the roses. A dreamy per-sonality fantasizing about life and love seldom produces results. Someone too reliant upon the five senses will pooh-pooh anything that cannot be seen or touched, missing out on new, innovative ideas. The psychic-active type who runs around willy-nilly, acting on hunches without a game plan, shoots his arrows at too many tar-gets. Each temperament in the right combination with other temperaments is the essence of creativity.

What would you identify as your primary tempera-ment? From most dominant to least dominant, how would you list your temperaments?

The Elements in Nature

The ancients believed that nature used all of the ele-ments in a variety of combinations to create the majestic harmony found in the natural environment. Carefully combining and balancing the elements is important so that one element does not destroy the others. This doesn't mean that the amount of each element is equal, but that there is an interplay of elements creating a dynamic equilibrium that prevents one element from dominating.

Water is essential for the growth of plants and sustenance of animals, but too much Water can erode the soil, flood the Earth, and even drown the inhabitants. The dampness of Water is naturally balanced by the warmth and dryness of the change in seasons together promoting healthy growth of plants and animals. Air is essential for all living things; too little Air results in suffocation and death. Too much Air dries out the Earth and either intensifies Fire or blows it out. Strong winds can whip seas into gigantic waves or touch off hurricane violence that destroys areas of the Earth. Earth provides a medium for plant growth and production of food, without which there is starvation and death. A temporary imbalance can cause droughts, floods, and fires. Fire is necessary as a catalyst to transform one element into another, to cook raw foods, to provide warmth from freezing temperatures, and as a natural purifying agent when forests need thinning. When Fire burns unchecked it can destroy shelter, prime forests, and animals. As you can see, each element has positive and negative characteristics. If not utilized in combination with other elements, the negative characteristics tend to be overpowering. Nature is a master teacher in the ingenious balance of elements, creating variety and change within a revolving cycle of repetitive rhythm. Whenever I am uncertain about whether I am on the right track I always rely on the principle of balance. Whether I'm designing for a client, deciding how to spend free time, or even mulling over various spiritual issues, this important principle guides me in my decision making. It's not surprising that along with the saying of "Know Thyself," over a sacred portal of Delphi was another inscription: "Nothing in Excess."

Diagrams of the Elements

When laid out in diagrammatical form, the four elements have been depicted as the points of an equal-armed cross, with the fifth element (Quintessence) located where the arms intersect. The cross as an X inside a circle is another symbol associated with the four elements and also the pyramid shape with the four elements represented on each corner and Quintessence as the top point. Another interesting symbolic association is the pentagram arranging the four basic elements on the four lower cusps and Spirit on the top cusp [fig. 20].

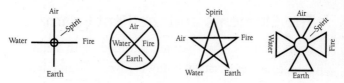

Figure 20

Each element had an opposite element and when laid out in a diagram they were positioned across from each other. The two adjacent elements were considered corresponding elements. Earth's opposite was Air, and Water's opposite Fire. Earth corresponded with Water and Fire. Air related to Fire and Water, etc. Two of the elements were considered feminine and two were masculine. Earth and Water were associated with feminine energies and were thought of as descending elements, as water flows downhill and earth's core is under the surface. Fire and Air were masculine, ascending elements (both Air and Fire rise).

Water combined with Earth creates an environment for fertile growth. Fire warms the chill of Air, but too much Water in a predominantly Fire environment negates it, while used in small quantities it can help to temper Fire's destructive powers. Too much Air combined with Earth creates dry, dusty conditions and eliminates moisture or stirs up Fire. Elements that are conducive to each other's development are considered corresponding elements—the others are opposing. Converse elements are used together sparingly, corresponding elements combine more easily.

The Elements and the Pentagram

The pentagram is a five-pointed star made with a continuous line. Its mystical number five is found frequently in nature: five fingers, five toes, five senses, five petals on many flowers, and five compartments in many fruits. In ancient Greece the number five (*pente*) was a symbol of the world and meant all or complete.

When the pentagram is en-
closed in a circle, it is surrounded by another sacred
symbol, and becomes a powerful icon for protection, associated with the goddess Kore, also
known as Ceres and Demeter
(Earth Mother) [fig. 21]. Inside
the pentagram is a pentagon, a
five-sided figure related to the
symbol for home (a square with
a triangle on top) [fig. 22].

Figure 21

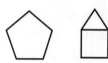

Figure 22

Greek mathematician Pythagoras claimed in the sixth century BCE that the pentagram was perfection in terms of geometry. It was closely associated with the four elements when perfectly balanced, with the fifth essence over all. Later adopted as the sign of brother-hood among the Pythagoreans, its sacred geometry was paramount in the construction of the Parthenon and the pyramids at Giza. The symbol was also found on potsherds in ancient Mesopotamia dated at 3500 BCE and on rings worn by Romans engraved with a coiled snake and a pentagram dedicated to the god-dess Salus (Hygeia). Druids called it the endless knot and honored it as a symbol of the Godhead. In me-dieval times it represented truth and security and was used above windows and doors as a protection from demons. It was revered during the Renaissance era by such renowned geniuses as Leonardo da Vinci, whose illustration of the Vitruvian Man correlates the shape of the pentagram to the perfection of the human form. In modern art, Piet Mondrian and Le Corbusier applied its geometric doctrine to their art and architecture. This sacred symbol, used by many well-respected scientists and artisans, was not associated with anything diabolical until the infamous Inquisition of the fourteenth century.

Again, when the pentagram is positioned so that one point is up, the upper point represents Spirit. Air and Fire are across the upper points (ascending), and Water and Earth are the lower two points (descending). The alignment and interconnectedness of the elements in the pentagram make it a perfect symbol for the spiritual home. The mathematics and geometrical proportions associated with the pentagram and the relationship to architecture and design have already aligned this symbol with the creative arts for millennia.

The Golden Ratio

The Golden Ratio is a mathematical principle used in architecture and the decorative arts as a rule of thumb for creating pleasing proportions. This seemingly insignificant term is actually a very profound principle. When a line is divided so that the ratio of the smaller segment to the larger segment is the same as the larger segment to the whole, the division is considered the Golden Section (sacred proportion, divine proportion, etc.) The two segments have a ratio of 1:1.615 known as the Golden Ratio. Numbers that relate to the Golden Ratio are called the Fibonacci numbers. This sequence of numbers: 1, 2, 3, 5, 8, 13, 21, 34, 55, etc., are created by the sum of the previous two numbers. They are called irrational numbers (irreducible fractions.) The ratio of 3 to 5 and 5 to 8 and 8 to 13, etc. approximates the Golden Ratio of 1: 1.615, where the larger the number in this sequence, the closer it comes to the actual Golden Ratio.

The Golden Ratio and Fibonacci number series is found in nature in surprising ways. The spiral (which can be constructed using the principles of the Golden Rectangle) is found in such disparate things as a nautilus, a nebula, a pine cone, a daisy, and the seed pod of a sunflower, and are all related to the Golden Ratio and the Fibonacci numbers. The pine cone has 8 spirals in one direction and 13 in the other; the daisy has 21 clockwise and 34 counterclockwise spirals. In botany, the intrinsic involvement in plant growth of these patterns is called *phyllotaxis*.

The proportions of the Golden Ratio form the geometrical basis for the Parthenon, considered by many architectural historians to be the most beautiful building in the world. Many architects and designers today employ these principles in creating harmonious proportions. For instance, when dividing a wall for the application of wall coverings and wainscoting, a typical 8- foot-high ceiling is often divided into two segments; 3 feet for one treatment and 5 feet for the other. All three numbers are Fibonacci numbers and the ratio of 3 to 5 is the same as 5 to 8 or 1:1.615 approximately. The same principle is being used when we say three pillows are more interesting than four, and room sizes are more pleasing the closer they come to the Golden Rectangle.

Relationship of the Pentagram to the Golden Section

Every straight line in the pentagram is divided into Golden Sections by the lines that cross them. The pentagram can be further divided into smaller and smaller pentagrams containing hundreds of divine relationships (Golden Ratios.) In Greece, the pentagram was also acknowledged as the *pentalpha*, or five As, with A symbolizing beginning or birth. The pentagram is also known as the triple triangle—the sacred shape plus the sacred number associated with the ancient Goddess.

The pentagram is associated with harmonious balance and a symbol of good health (the name of the goddess of health, Hygeia, was inscribed on the pentagram used by the Pythagoreans). When we create harmonious balance in our living spaces we contribute to our own good health mentally, emotionally, physically, psychically, and spiritually.

Eurhythmy

The Greeks called the harmonious relationship symbolized by the pentagram *eurhythmy* (eurhythmic). According to the Greeks, eurhythmy was not only linked to music, but had a much wider interpretation. Art and architecture, the performing arts, in fact all of humankind's creations should be eurhythmic. Music, art, architecture, and interiors should be created without too much similarity or repetition, with enough contrast to be interesting but organized according to some overall theme or agreement among parts. In other words, all parts should relate to the whole in a rhythmic beat that is varied to avoid monotony, has contrast to provide stimulation, and is held together with a common melody to prevent chaos. In interior design, eurhythmy means the creation of free-flowing, unique, yet harmonious space—with movement from one room to another and within each room that not only carries the eye around the area but generates a kind of vitality as well.

The principle of eurhythmy occurs when elements are balanced, vital spirit is present, and there is a cohesive overall feeling of harmony that creates flow. Interior space treated in this way feels vibrant, and vibrancy literally is what is created. Particles vibrate and the air is filled with life, colors dance, and pools of light feel sacred. Your home becomes alive and interactive, providing a mutual support. As you tenderly nurture your personal space, your home reciprocates with a nurturing atmosphere to support you.

To summarize, the four elements—Air, Water, Earth, and Fire—infused with Spirit and combined in various pleasing proportions, provide a balanced, vital, harmonious atmosphere. When these elements are thus combined in our homes, the quality of eurhythmy (the rhythmic flowing of energy) is evident in the essence of what can truly be called our *living spaces!*

---

1 Walker, *Women's Encyclopedia*, 273.
2 Opsopaus, John, "The Ancient Greek Esoteric Doctrine of the Elements," http://www.notaccess.com/RELATIONSHIPS/GeometryAL.htm, 1998.

Chapter 7

Archetypal Design Styles

In sacred space, everything is done so that the environment becomes a metaphor.[1]

Joseph Campbell

Creating Harmony

Have you ever wondered why some people are able to put things together and they just seem perfect? Their clothes and homes are always tasteful. How did they know what seemingly unrelated things would work so well together? Were they just born with a knack for it? Some people probably are born with an inherent sense of style, but the rest of us can learn. Maybe you were like me and at some point in your early childhood someone really savvy, an older sister perhaps, clued you in on proper taste in clothes. I can remember my older sister saying something like, "That blouse doesn't go with that skirt," or "Yuk, those two patterns clash." Maybe you were one of the fortunate who seemed to create your own style that was quirky and fun, but never tacky. The rest of us needed some pointers. However we learned, we most likely now know as adults that a frilly sheer blouse and long dangling rhinestone earrings don't look right with a wool plaid blazer, or a business suit calls for more formal foot attire than white sox and penny loafers. The same principles are at work in putting together your home. Certain styles work well with lots of unusual and disparate accessories. Others seem to call for more simplistic, minimal additions.

Each time we add something to our home it affects the overall scheme. When we pay attention to nature, we see unique and ever-changing design patterns. Flowers and trees change shape and color, and blend or contrast harmoniously with other elements, depending upon the various seasons. This is the same principle used when organizing the various elements in our homes into unified patterns. We want to use enough variety to be interesting, but maintain enough commonality to avoid chaos. A home that is aesthetically pleasing is like good music or beautiful art; it makes you feel good. A home that is beautiful and functional and a true inspiration to its owners is not haphazardly thrown together, but rather created with love, either intuitively or with study and planning, laid out in a manner that takes into account all the variables and reconciles the differences with the overall theme, pulling it all together into a cohesive creation.

Ancient architects knew that all manmade creations were composed of the same elements as in nature. They also knew the elements must be treated with the same respect. Art, architecture, and design had rules and guidelines for combining elements. Too much of one element can destroy equilibrium. In design terms, not enough variation appears trite, whereas too much feels chaotic. The eminent architecture of the classical age taught us a great deal about good design. In our built environment we need to be adept at rhythmically using one element as repetition with associated elements as variety, and small amounts of the opposing element as contrast in order to create harmonious results. It's much like creating a melody. First there needs to be an underlying theme with a repetitive beat, but to keep it from being too monotonous we introduce a variation of the original beat, plus a range of notes, then to bring in an exciting change of pace, perhaps a clash of cymbals for emphasis. You've probably heard tunes that are so repetitious and boring you immediately want to turn them off. In a home this is analogous to a matching suite of furniture with coordinated fabrics, and certainly some music gets carried away by introducing so much variety that you wonder what the melody is. In design, this is like a home that is so eclectic nothing seems to relate to anything else.

Eurhythmy is a rhythmic harmony achieved by using subtle variations and change of tempo, incorporating small opposing traits for contrast, while keeping the whole concept aligned with a single predominant element. What we're talking about is a home that has agreement among parts, but is not so perfect that it feels wrong to move anything because the equilibrium might be destroyed. There is a wide latitude of choice in creating harmonious interiors. A very eclectic style where variety abounds might appeal to you; or you might prefer a more cohesive setting with greater repetition of similar patterns, colors, and styles. The important thing is what feels comfortable to you, not what is in vogue. Using the elements in unique, yet balanced, ways is the ultimate goal.

Unique Characteristics
of Each Element

Whatever building materials and interior furnishings we bring into our homes affects the overall balance. By choosing and identifying the characteristics of one element (or combination) we can create an overall theme. These themes can then be interspersed with compatible traits from other elements for variety and balance. Awareness of the identifying characteristics of each element allows us to make adjustments using more variety or more similarity as needed. As in nature, a long-term imbalance in our homes can result in unhealthy conditions.

The four elements (plus Spirit) are closely aligned with design. If we gather together the various characteristics of each element, a design style emerges. For example, Water's damp nature is associated with colors and materials that are indicative of its properties: blues, lavenders, and cool greens, smooth reflective materials, glass, mirrors, and bubbling fountains. Assigned gender qualities of feminine for Water and Earth and masculine for Fire and Air further define the styles. When we add their respective temperaments, an even broader picture is painted. The elements are now enlivened with archetypal images. Feminine Water is associated with emotions, dreams, and love and becomes Venus, the Tarot Priestess, a fairy princess, Isis, Aphrodite, or the Lady of the Lake.

As we define the four archetypal design styles associated with the four elements, deeper and more complex images will come to mind. These archetypal associations have subconscious significance; each character reminds us of myths and folk tales with personal and universal symbolism. Creating various styles will no longer be a mystery. Archetypal styles will awaken pictures in your subconscious memory, making it so much easier to identify and incorporate the desirable traits of each one.

As we become familiar with the four archetypal styles, we can combine them with other compatible styles for more variety, or balance them with additional traits from other elements. In design, the predominance of one style creates a theme, something cohesive to hold together all the various parts, just as in nature where the theme is set by the season, or geographical location. The predominant theme balanced with qualities of other elements in lesser degrees creates a congruous result. This then is our intended goal: to create a harmonious design that is reflective of the beauty of nature where elements balance each other in a lively dance of equilibrium.

You will most likely find yourself more drawn to one of two of these styles, or perhaps a combination of

Figure 23

two styles. This will enable you to define your own personal style. Knowing your individual preference is vital when creating an environment that is designed to appeal to your unique personality. Over the passageway at Delphi the words "Know Thyself" are as important today as they were thousands of years ago. To be able to create a personal sanctuary, you must know what surroundings you are attracted to and those that give you the nurturing feeling your home is meant to bring.

Water: The Priestess

When we create interiors in our homes, we use the actual elements themselves, and also representations of those elements. For instance, we might build a house on a cliff overlooking the ocean, or create a waterfall or fountain within view of the living areas of the home. These are examples of actual Water elements. We can also add Water by using materials that look or feel like Water. Glossy surfaces, reflective metals, glass, and sheer, shimmery fabrics psychologically remind us of Water. Using colors associated with Water, cool blues, grays, pale blue greens, cool violets, and bluish whites create a watery atmosphere. Water corresponds to cups, hearts, and the Zodiac signs Pisces, Cancer, and Scorpio. As a design style, Water is formal, feminine, and romantic.

As previously mentioned, Water archetypes are the Lady of the Lake, Aphrodite, a fairy princess, or the Tarot Priestess. These archetypes bring to mind pictures and stories that can illicit deep memories and universal associations. For example, we can envision the priestess living in a temple made of alabaster and

The High Priestess
The Universal Tarot, © Lo Scarabeo

limestone overlooking the sea, with fountains flowing in the courtyard where she sits on a marble bench, dressed in a diaphanous white gown. She appears cool and serene, but she is a classic romantic at heart. She is a temple goddess who uses Water as a purification ritual in her holy duties. Her boudoir is opulent with satin sheets and sumptuous, gauzy fabrics draping her bed; a large marble sunken tub, pedestal sinks, and walls of mirror furnish the adjacent bath. The moon and its silvery light are welcome guests in her chambers, casting an iridescent glow over the smooth, refined materials. She is Isis and Athena.

If she lived today, her choice of homes might be a neoclassical mansion, a Paris apartment, or a Mediterranean villa, and perhaps all three. She loves to entertain formally with crystal and china on her table of glass or highly polished wood, where a striking formal floral arrangement in a Baccarat crystal vase might grace the center. Her living room furnishings are predominantly white or a soft tint with pale clear, cool colors as accents. She is spring, the budding of new shoots promising rebirth and the palest of colors whispering of gay flowers yet to bloom. She is the fertile potential of rebirth and regeneration.

Earth: Earth Mother

Earth style is feminine and informal, known for its tactile, visual, auditory, and aromatic sensations. Earth archetypes are Gaea, Hera, Mother Nature, Juno and

Demeter—the mother aspect of the Triple Goddess. She carries wheat, a child, or the horn of plenty. She lives in a cottage or simple home, perhaps with painted shutters and a white, rose-covered picket fence. Furnishings are simple yet inviting; overstuffed chairs covered with checks or plaids and colorful stylized flo-

The Empress
The Universal Tarot, © Lo Scarabeo

ral patterns. Area rugs are casually strewn on her wooden or stone floors. Her kitchen has small-paned windows opening to her lush garden of vegetables, herbs, and flowers. She is a healer and lives closely in touch with nature. Birds, pets, and children are welcomed to her cozy cottage, where the smell of freshly baked bread permeates the air. She is drawn to painted cabinets and furniture rather than dark woods or synthetic material. Her season is summer and the warm colors and flowers of summer are dear to her. Her tarot suit is pentacles and card suit is diamonds, representing the abundance of nature and prosperity in the physical domain.

Many of the furnishings and finish materials in our homes are made of natural materials representing Earth. Stone, rock, brick, concrete, adobe, and stucco are common Earth materials used in construction. Fireplaces, countertops, walls, floors and exterior foundations are typically made of Earth materials. Earth elements lend strength, stability, long-lasting quality, and perceived value to our homes. On a metaphysical level, they help to ground us.

Earth elements also represent the bounty of the garden; flowers, fruits, and herbs, fresh or in patterns, belong here. Colors are a combination of natural, earthy browns, various greens, and muted warm tints such as apricot or peach, with colorful accents of floral hues.

Fire: Magician

The archetype for Fire is the Magician, a Druid, Merlin, and Odin. He is a shapeshifter and a trickster. His shamanic associations connect him to Hermes, the messenger between the two worlds—the earth plane and the lower world. He is closely associated with the tree of life. Odin hung from it for nine days to gain the wisdom of the other world. Merlin retreated to his beloved forest living in trees. Druids worshipped in their sacred groves and their name was derived from the Greek word for oak (*drus*). The wizard's wand is fashioned from yew wood.

In design terminology, the Magician (Fire) is informal, and loves natural woods and rough-woven fabrics. He would feel at home in a log cabin, chalet, or an Arts and Crafts bungalow, originally designed by Magician-type idealists. This style of architecture is known for its humble size and style, yet built with integrity using the finest quality woodworking skills. The furnishings are solid oak, dear to the Magician, with substantial joinery; medieval tapestry or leafy forest designs cover the cushions. His surroundings are simple yet functional; a fireplace essential. His season is autumn and the colors that are associated with that season: warm browns, russet, oranges, gold, and warm reds. Greens are muted and yellowed with the passing of summer's heat. He prefers a country home, but if in the city, he chooses casual furnishings and warm, natural materials, leaning toward leather and hides, simple geometric patterns, denim, and nubby solids.

The Magician allies with the Tarot suit wands and card suit clubs. He is active and creative: the artisan, builder, and outdoorsman.

The Magician
The Universal Tarot, © Lo Scarabeo

Air: Warrior / King

The sky gods: Zeus, Thor, Jupiter, and Jove are associated with thunder and lightning and the masculine element Air. They are powerful rulers who cut to the chase. Air is the sword in Tarot and the spade in playing cards. A sky god-type prefers clean lines and metallic finishes reminiscent of his sword, Excalibur. He favors contemporary minimalist design, severe contrasts, and strong, deep jewel tones. His tastes in furnishings include glass and chrome tables, and modern classics: black leather chairs with aluminum or chrome legs such as Meis van der Rohe's Barcelona chair or Le Corbusier's chaise lounge. He is happiest in a penthouse apartment in a major city like New York or an industrial loft minimally furnished with over-scaled contemporary artwork and a view of the skyline from undraped windows. His intellect, no-nonsense attitude and respect for technology is apparent in his selection of clean-lined and sleek furnishings and materials. His design dictum: "Less is more."

A prototype of a more traditional Air style is medieval lore's King Arthur. He is at home in a stone castle dressed in a purple, ermine-lined robe, his sword and scabbard, his most prized possessions, by his side. He craves openness and thus locates his lofty castle with grand-scaled rooms on a mountaintop close to his beloved sky.

Air represents mental attributes and scientific thinking. His season is winter. The stark winter landscape dictates his color palette: black and white or neutral, with accents of strong, deep, intense, cool hues.

The Emperor
The Universal Tarot, © Lo Scarabeo

In today's homes, Air qualities give an open, airy feeling to an enclosed space; large picture windows with sweeping views of the horizon, minimal furnishings and accessories, large open rooms with high ceilings, unpatterned fabrics, and clean-lined furniture. This open, breezy atmosphere is the opposite of the cluttered intimate feel of Earth.

Which archetype most appeals to you? Does that archetype define anything about your temperament? Are there any styles that you really dislike?

Summary of Archetypal Design Styles

Water

Archetypes: Priestess (Isis, Aphrodite, Venus, fairy princess, Lady of the Lake, Athena)
Tarot: Cups
Card Suit: Hearts
Zodiac Signs: Pisces, Cancer, Scorpio
Season: Spring
Temperament & Personality Style: feeling, idealist, romantic
Design Elements: Feminine Formal
  Style: Romantic
  Colors: cool tints (cool light blues, grays, pale aqua, lavender, bluish whites)
  Patterns: wavy lines, curves, naturalistic floral patterns

Textures & Fabrics: smooth, sheer, shimmery, gauzy, silk, satin, lace

Building Materials: glass, marble, limestone, reflective metals

Furnishings: French and classical style furniture, down-filled white sofas

Queen of Chalices
The Universal Tarot, © Lo Scarabeo

Architecture: Neoclassical mansion,
  Mediterranean villa, southern plantation, Paris
  apartment
Symbols & Artifacts: fish, frog, shells, wavy
lines, water birds, water lilies, mermaid, heart,
  water snakes, sea glass, iris, hyacinth, etc.
Symbols Represent: relationships, dreams,
  emotions, romance, fertility

Earth

Archetypes: Earth Mother (Gaea, Hera, Demeter,
  Juno)
Tarot: Pentacles, Coins
Card Suit: Diamonds
Zodiac Signs: Taurus, Virgo, Capricorn
Season: Summer
Temperament & Personality Style: sensing, nurtur-
  ing, guardian
Design Elements: Feminine Informal
  Style: Country and cottage styles
  Colors: warm tints (natural earth colors, warm
    light greens, yellow, apricot, peach, coral and
    colorful accents of floral hues)
  Patterns: stylized floral patterns, checks, plaids
  Textures & Fabrics: natural, home-spun, cotton,
    linen
  Building Materials: stone, rock, adobe, stucco,
    painted wood
  Furnishings: overstuffed chairs, slip covers,
    painted wood tables

Architecture: cottage, simple bungalow

Symbols & Artifacts: circles, fruits, flowers, rocks, salt, wheat, horn of plenty, seeds, crystals, coins, herbs, etc.

Symbols Represent: abundance and prosperity

Queen of Pentacles
The Universal Tarot, © Lo Scarabeo

Fire

Archetypes: Magician (Merlin, Odin, Druids, Hermes)
Tarot: Wands
Card Suit: Clubs
Zodiac Signs: Aries, Leo, Sagittarius

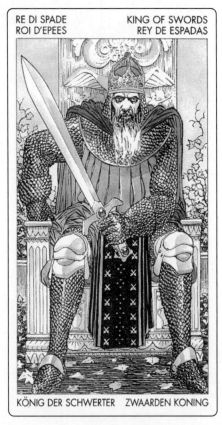

King of Swords
The Universal Tarot, © Lo Scarabeo

Season: Autumn

Temperament & Personality Style: intuition, artisan, outdoors person

Design Elements: Masculine Informal

  Style: Ethnic, Western, Arts and Crafts style

  Colors: warm shades (red, russet, orange, gold, warm green, warm brown)

  Patterns: geometrics, leaves and forest patterns, flame stitch

  Textures & Fabrics: rough-hewn, rugged, leather, hides, denim

  Building Materials: natural wood, especially oak and ash, wrought iron

  Furnishings: Oak tables and chairs, log furniture, hand-hewn, ethnic, tribal

  Architecture: Arts and Crafts bungalow, log cabin, ranch, chalet

  Symbols & Artifacts: sun, wheel, cross, trees, acorns, wands, candles, Phoenix, salamander, etc.

  Symbols Represent: creativity, protection

Air

Archetypes: Warrior/king (Zeus, Thor, Jupiter, Jove, King Arthur)

Tarot: Swords

Card Suit: Spades

Zodiac Signs: Aquarius, Gemini, Libra

Season: Winter

Temperament & Personality Style: thinking,
  rational, warrior
Design Elements: Masculine Formal
  Style: contemporary—high tech or traditional—
  opulent

Knight of Swords
The Universal Tarot, © Lo Scarabeo

Colors: cool shades (strong deep jewel tones, black and white, strong contrasts)

Patterns: abstract, solids

Textures & Fabrics: contemporary—smooth, plush, black leather or traditional—tapestries, brocades, velvets

Building Materials: contemporary—metal, synthetics or traditional—stone

Architecture: contemporary—modern, minimalist or traditional—castle

Furnishings: contemporary—clean lines, sleek, high tech or traditional—large scale, ornate

Symbols & Artifacts: eagles, hawks, vertical lines, zigzags, Tau cross, sword shapes, feathers, thunderbolts, lightning, obelisk, angel, etc.

Symbols Represent: ideas, intellectual pursuits, inner warrior

Combining Elements

If we only had one season, life would be boring; and the earth would not be able to recycle the old and introduce the new. In our homes, having just one major element can also become boring and predictable. The overall ambiance can be too cold or too hot, too dry or too wet. We need to combine other elements for balance. The opposing elements are more difficult to combine than corresponding or correlating elements. Fire and Water are opposing elements, as are Earth and Air. Fire and Earth or Fire and Air are correlating; as are Water and Air or Water and Earth. As you think of nature, imagine going directly from winter to summer without the transition of spring. There is too much contrast. If two partners occupying the same house are opposite elements, the situation is more difficult. Working with hundreds of clients over more than twenty years, I know from experience that creating a successful design scheme with two opposing elements takes a lot of compromise!

Earth and Air

Let's take a set of opposing elements as an example. Earth is casual, feminine, and abundant; Air is staid, masculine, and minimal. Earth is cozy and comfortable, filled with flowers and patterns, whereas Air is unpatterned, open, and aloof. Too much Earth is dusty and cluttered; too much Air is cold and sterile. To bring an opposite element into a design scheme, one must use caution. Earth can be brought into Air by using natural stone or granite countertops rather than metal or synthetics, or by using plants, trees, or fresh flowers to add life to a too-sterile environment. In a stuffy Earth atmosphere, adding a recirculating fan or opening windows to catch the breeze, organizing and eliminating excess clutter, and dusting collections of meaningful objects are ways of airing out the space.

Fire and Water

Fire and Water are also opposites. Fire's wood surfaces, natural-textured patterns, and masculine informality contradict Water's feminine formal, cool, sleek materials. Warming a too-cool, watery atmosphere with candles or a fireplace could add just the right touch. You can also refresh a hot stuffy Fire atmosphere with water misted in the air or vases with water and flowers. Masculine informal (Fire) is hard to mix with feminine formal (Water), just as masculine formal (Air) is quite alien from feminine informal (Earth). Trying to add half Fire and half Water or half Earth and half Air is doomed to failure, as the Water will squelch the Fire and too much Air will dry out the Earth.

Earth and Fire

On the other hand, elements next to each other mix much more easily. Fire and Earth share informality. Earth's feminine nature blended with Fire's masculine one neutralize genders. An overabundance of flowers and too many knicknacks give way to stylized simple patterns, straight-lined geometrics, and larger-scale furnishings. Natural fibers and textures and possibly ethnic motifs work well in an Earth/Fire style. The results are warm, earthy, and informal, and neither too sweet nor too masculine.

Water and Earth

When Water and Earth mix, the style is feminine but not as formal as Water and not as informal as Earth— perhaps a Cape Cod-style home or a Federal tradition- al style. Floral patterns are more likely to be chintzes, more formal than the cottage, but less formal and ro- mantic than the sheer, shimmery fabrics of Water. Ac- cessories include floral paintings, vases of flowers, and polished wood surfaces, but the style is neither too country nor too formal.

Fire and Air

Fire and Air combinations add warmth to the coolness of winter and bring fresh air to the hot stuffiness of too much Fire. A country estate or townhouse, with a pan- eled den containing trophies from fishing or hunting excursions, or a library lined with leatherbound books furnished with tables and desks of polished dark woods, and leather or tapestry-covered wing chairs defines this combination. The feeling is semiformal and definitely masculine.

Air and Water

Air and Water are both cool and sleek, with the femi- nine nature of Water easing the hard edges of mas- culine Air. Large picture windows, gleaming floors, furnishings with sumptuous, cool-colored fabrics and overscaled accessories in a lofty great room opening to a kitchen with granite or solid surface countertops and stainless steel appliances is an example of an Air/Water combination.

Summary of Blends

In summation, when the two masculine styles merge the result is masculine semiformal (the informality of Fire blending with the formality of Air). Likewise the two feminine styles become feminine and moderately informal. A masculine and feminine style together is neutral gender and either formal (Air/Water) or informal (Earth/Fire).

Combining Design Styles

Water / Air

Archetypes: Priestess and King

Design Elements: Formal/neutral gender (neither too feminine nor too masculine)

Style: regal and refined

Colors: cool (tints and shades) various blues, violet, white, gray

Patterns: stripes, formal floral and tapestries

Textures & Fabrics: smooth, plush, velvets, satins, silk

Building Materials: granite, marble, polished tight-grained wood

Furnishings: elegant, classical, heavily carved or clean lined with sumptuous fabrics

Architecture: formal classical mansions, grand scale, open floor plans

Water / Earth

Archetypes: Priestess and Earth Mother

Design Elements: Feminine/semi formal (neither too formal nor too informal)

Style: relaxed feminine (Shabby Chic style is a typical Water/Earth combination)

Colors: combination of warm and cool tints

Patterns: florals, stripes and solids

Textures & Fabrics: soft, natural textures, chintz, linen, cotton

Building materials: wood, stone

Furnishings: upholstered sofas and chairs in relaxed fabrics, combinations of wood and glass tables

Architecture: wide range of styles: Victorian, Cape Cod, Queen Anne etc.

Earth / Fire

Archetypes: Earth Mother and Magician

Design Elements: Informal/neutral gender (neither too feminine nor too masculine)

Style: Country

Colors: warm colors both tints and shades

Patterns: combinations of geometrics and stylized florals

Textures & Fabrics: natural, nubby, cotton, denim, textured linen

Building Materials: wood (painted and natural) and stone

Furnishings: casual combinations of upholstered pieces and wood tables

Architecture: informal styles such as cabins or bungalows

Fire / Air

Archetypes: Magician And King

Design Elements: Masculine/semi-formal

Style: country estate, gentleman rancher

Colors: combinations of cool and warm shades

Patterns: geometrics, stripes, solids

Textures & Fabrics: combinations of smooth and plush; leather, wool

Building Materials: wood, dark polished, either tight or open-grained, granite, stone

Furnishings: larger scaled furniture, wing chairs, leather sofas, wood tables, bookcases, libraries

Architecture: large ranch style home, English country estate

Combining More Than Two Styles

Combining more than two styles is certainly possible, but with caution because one of the three styles will be an opposite. For example, Water and Earth combine to become a feminine, less formal style, possibly with down-pillowed sofas and flowery fabrics. Adding a fireplace or perhaps a room that is more masculine, such as a den or library, introduces Fire, ceiling fans to circulate stuffy air brings in that element. Ideally something from each of the four categories should be introduced into each room, but in the case of opposites, using small amounts, or items brought out for certain occasions, creates just the right touch.

Does a blend of two styles come closer to defining your favorite style than just one particular element?

Bringing in the Missing Elements

Whatever design style we choose, bringing the missing elements into our space is essential for equilibrium. The majority of present day homes have an over abundance of certain elements and a lack of others. For example, electrical appliances (Air) are major features in today's homes, adding excessive electrical energy. Telephones, fax machines, televisions, computers, hair dryers, dishwashers, food processors, mixers, blenders, garbage disposals, vacuum cleaners, lighting, heating, air conditioning, washing machines, dryers, and all of the other power tools and labor-saving devices we moderns own create an imbalance similar to a dry electrical storm. Imagine a sustained, massive storm lighting the sky with electrical currents, a lightning storm without rain. This is what the interior environments of our homes are like with the contemporary use of too many electrical appliances. Now, if during the electrical storm Fires are started, we observe a natural occurrence that helps clean the brush and dead wood from diseased forests. Finally, when the rain arrives (Water) to quell the Fire and dampen the Earth, the soil is made rich with nutrients from the ashes and the water. This, then, is the balance of nature, using an interchange of elements in varying degrees to bring about homeostasis.

Too Much Water

When a house is dominated by one element it feels much like one season, year after year. For example, if the whole house is predominantly Water, it can feel too cold and damp; especially unwelcome when the outside weather is the same. Certain locations on the ocean, for instance, tend to have not only a predominant water view, but a great deal of foggy weather as well, creating a large expanse of gray. What one would think would be a "dream house" can be a dreary one instead. Earth touches are especially helpful to warm up and dry out this "too damp" scenario.

My former design partner's house has solid walls of glass, with a spectacular vista of a swimming pool that appears to flow over the hillside into the river below. The large-scaled rooms with high ceilings and floors of limestone add to the Water element. To compensate for what could be too much water, we furnished the home with large pieces of comfortable upholstered furniture, using an inviting color palette that included warmer accent colors, and incorporated plush, patterned area rugs to soften the hard surface of the flooring.

Too Much Air

Air dwellings may have a preponderance of artificial surfaces. Products imitating natural materials often lack the patina or character of the real thing. Interiors with too many synthetic surfaces can feel sterile and laboratory-like, even artificial. Wood surfaces (Fire) or granite, limestone, or marble (Water) can be introduced, adding warmth and character to an overly artificial space.

Quite often this design style is associated with the workplace. Many contemporary office buildings have interiors that feel cold and impersonal. This no-nonsense attitude is part of the Air image of cutting to the core or getting rid of excessive frills. Many people who work in an atmosphere of this nature are literally "out of their own element." Bringing a plant or picture from home and a few important symbolic artifacts can help to personalize your office space.

Too Much Fire

An example of too much Fire is a log cabin with wood walls and floors, wood furnishings, naturalistic patterns such as leaves, warm colors on fabrics, dark wood or metal antique accessories, and a large fireplace as a focal point. The house is dark, warm, and suffocating. Colors, pattern, plants and flowers, and fresh circulated air through shiny windows will help immensely to balance this hot, stuffy house.

Our cabin in the Northwest was originally made up of too many Fire elements. The small living room had both a used-brick fireplace that was not in use and a free-standing, wood-burning stove. The exterior and interior living areas were lined with cedar boards, and the tiny kitchen, open to the living room, was finished with yellow pine cabinets and white walls.

Initially we decorated the cabin with items we had on hand, antique accessories made of wood or iron from my husband's previous antique importing business. The few winter months we spent there felt warm and cozy, but the summer months were not as pleasant. The dominant Fire element gave the cabin a dark, stuffy atmosphere. Soon we replaced the free-standing stove with an insert in the previously unused fireplace, eliminating a major Fire element from the living room. One summer I brought a floral chair from our primary home. At first it looked out of place in the masculine style of the mountain cabin, but I decided instead of recovering it, to introduce more items with a cottage (Earth) feeling to cheer up the cabin's somber atmosphere. I painted the kitchen light sage green, added colorful striped and floral pillows to the sofa, covered the floor with a patterned area rug, and bought a few indoor plants. The cabin now has a combination Earth/ Fire setting. The cheerful colors and summer flowers add a welcome touch of femininity to a once too-hot, too-masculine setting.

Too Much Earth

A home with too much Earth can appear cluttered, chaotic, and "cutesy." Too many patterns and colors can become confusing, and too many "home sweet home" objects appear trite and sticky sweet. My husband disdainfully labels an overabundance of Earth style as "Ducks with Bows." Cupboards that are open to display patterned dishes can be charming unless they are crowded and chaotic. Too much Earth in an interior is like a garden gone to seed. End tables filled with so many dainty tea cups that there's no functional place to set a glass, homemade wooden cut-outs of barnyard animals, or a plethora of floral paintings adorning the walls without any place to rest your eyes, and pillows of every imaginable floral pattern covering the furniture, making seating cumbersome, are typical ways of overdoing Earth elements.

As you look through shelter magazines, see if you can identify interiors that have too much of any one element. Does your own home have a preponderance of one element? Does it feel imbalanced?

Adding Missing Elements

In a well-balanced home, we will find each of the elements present, even if in very small amounts. The elements might vary with the seasons, for example during different times of the year we might add more of the element represented in that particular season, such as fresh flowers in summer or warming candles and a fire in the fireplace during chilly autumn evenings. Rolling up wool rugs and using summer slipcovers to lighten up the home for warmer seasons is a great way to imitate the variety of nature, and using seasonal holiday decorations creates periodic changes that ease the monotony of one elemental style all year long.

Following are some suggestions for adding missing elements to create balance, especially in homes where too much of one element predominates, or a combination of elements are desired.

Adding Fire Elements

A simple way to add more Fire to a room is to paint it a warm, rich color, such as red, gold, or terra cotta. Another way is to use natural stained wood products, especially oak or ash, whether in wall paneling, flooring, and/or furnishings. Rough-hewn materials like black or rusted wrought iron, dark-finished antique fixtures, and bookshelves filled with leatherbound books are great ways of adding warmth. Covering furniture in leather or nubby natural fabrics, and using geometric patterns or forest symbols like acorns and leaves as motifs also brings this element home. Most obviously, adding a fireplace is a very traditional and soulful way of adding Fire to your home. In lieu of this, using candles is an easy and inexpensive substitute. Burning aromatherapy candles or incense can literally fire you up, adding inspiration and passion to your life!

Adding Water Elements

There are several ingenious ways to add Water to your indoor environments. For instance, you can incorporate a small indoor water fountain, or position a courtyard or garden fountain close to living room or family room views. Aquariums add Water and movement to dry static rooms, as do glass vases filled with clear water and fresh flowers. In some particularly dry climates you might need a humidifier. Spraying the air with aromatic water is an easy way to bring this soothing element inside. Washing countertops, hard-surface flooring, and windows also incorporates a feeling of renewal that comes with refreshing Water energy. Glass or other shiny surfaces and gleaming, polished furniture provide a reflective quality associated with Water.

Painting walls with watery colors; lavenders, pale blues, and cool whites, and using soft, diaphanous materials at the windows will psychologically contribute to watering down hot spots. When we have too much clutter, or dusty dull surfaces, often found in homes with strong Earth or Fire elements, we need Water as a cleansing agent for renewal.

If you have a backyard swimming pool, bringing its effect indoors can be accomplished by adding glass patio doors or opening window treatments to allow the view. In our previous home, a beautiful courtyard pool was hidden behind louvered shutters covering an old metal sliding glass door. By replacing the sliding door with French doors, providing a view of the pool from the living room, we were able to add the missing Water element to our home, giving the entire house a new, refreshing appearance.

Adding Earth Touches

Earth can be brought into a home by adding things that are experienced by the five senses: touch, taste, sight, sound, and smell. Any realtor will tell you that a home sells more quickly if you have something wonderful cooking in the oven like fresh bread or cookies. I know we don't all have time in our busy schedules for baking bread, but using a tiny drop of aromatherapy oil on a lamp bulb or putting a bit of vanilla in a warm oven does wonders for the aromatic essence of your home.

Good music is essential in creating a healing sanctuary. The steady drone of negativity and fear produced by television does just the opposite. One delightful way of incorporating Earth sounds is to play recorded background music of nature such as birds singing in a meadow and water flowing over rocks. These tapes and CDs are easily found at most major audio stores or nature outlets.

For adding textural interest you can display shells, rocks, feathers, pine cones, and other natural materials in a basket or bowl. Varying tactile materials so everything is not smooth or shiny and incorporating some natural materials like slate, stone, or rock brings Earth's textures inside.

Ideally you may have views of nature from your home. Even a small balcony in a city apartment can contain potted plants, trees, flowers, and herbs, if only in the summer. A bird feeder in the winter can serve the same purpose. Indoor plants, fresh flowers, and pets add living elements to seemingly dead space. Landscape photography and paintings psychologically bring the outdoors in.

Authentic Earth tastes come with home-cooked food, something we have abandoned for fast foods, frozen microwave dinners, easy take-out, and delicatessen foods. One of the best things we can do for ourselves and our family is to cook nutritious food. On a cold winter day, nothing is more satisfying to the soul than a pot of soup or stew simmering on the stove.

Adding Air

Bringing in fresh air and recirculating existing air are essential to providing good Air quality in our manufactured environments. Our interior air is probably more polluted than the outside air. Without movement, air gets stagnant and trapped in indoor spaces, making our interior environment unhealthy. Food odors, dust, garbage, off-gassing of wallcoverings, paint, or carpeting, molds, and mildew are common air pollutants found in our homes. Whenever possible open windows to circulate air or use a fan to keep stagnant air moving. The obvious solution to dust, garbage, mildew, and molds and is frequent cleaning.

Purifying a space was a sacred act practiced in Roman temples before other rituals were performed. There was even a broom goddess named Devera (most likely where the later association with the witch and broom came from). When we clean our homes we can also create a ritual surrounding the task. For instance, I like to play sacred music, light a candle (usually a good quality aromatherapy candle), and if the weather permits, open doors and windows while I dust and vacuum my home. This surprisingly takes the drudgery out of most household chores. Adding a few drops of good quality aromatic essential oils to a spray bottle filled with water, then spritzing each room as you finish cleaning is a great way to freshen stale air and add the Water element as well. (More on this in chapter 9.)

If your home feels drafty, impersonal, and uninviting, you may be using too many Air elements. An apartment with steel and chrome furnishings and appliances, hard surface flooring, cool colors, and a view of the skyline can often feel bleak because of the cold, austere qualities of too much Air essence. Bringing in plants, warmer colors, and heavier textures and materials can help balance and ground a cool, airy space.

What other ways can you think of to add missing elements to your own home?

Building Materials

Wood, although primarily associated with Fire, is used in almost all housing construction materials such as framing, cabinetry, flooring, or furnishings. Typical Fire elements call for oak or ash with medium stain. Earth styles usually include lighter woods such as pine, or painted wood surfaces. The more formal Water styles utilize woods with highly reflective surfaces and little graining like cherry or fruitwood. Air uses exotic woods such as ebony or other dark, shiny woods for high contrast.

Of all the styles, Air uses less wood and more metal or synthetic materials. Sometimes even exposed metal girders are used to create this type of home style. Water styles prefer sleek surfaces: limestone, marble, or glass over wood.

To summarize, choosing one element or a combination of two associated elements as the predominant theme will help you select compatible materials, furnishings, colors, and patterns. Adding variety from one or more corresponding elements and a touch of contrast from the opposing element creates harmony. Once you begin to recognize the properties of each element, you will evaluate your home in a different manner. Imbalances will be easier to detect and remedy, and creating your own harmonious and well-balanced personal design style will be fun and exciting, rather than overwhelming.

Does your current space reflect elements from your favorite archetypal style? How might you bring aspects of that archetype into your home? Do you need to add balance by incorporating aspects of the other elements?

---

1 Osbon, 185.

Chapter 8

Calling Spirit Home

To live in sacred space is to live in a symbolic environment where spiritual life is possible,
where everything around you speaks of exalta-
tion of the spirit.[1]

Joseph Campbell

Quintessence (Spirit)

Quintessence, the fifth element, is the purest and most
essential element, according to the ancient Greeks, yet
it is the missing component in most contemporary
homes. When this aspect is overlooked, all other elements lack vitality. Dull, lifeless surroundings, artificial
lighting, too many electrical appliances, drab materials,
and stale air are common culprits that rob our homes
of vital energy. Many people feel that the place they
thought would fulfill their basic needs is instead a lifeless black hole, sucking their life blood instead of re-
plenishing their souls. Just thinking about all the work

required to take care of their home makes them tired. To these many people home has come to mean endless labor; a cycle of constant upkeep, replacement, and remodeling, with no end in sight, robbing them of precious energy and money.

Rather than feeling burdensome, your dwelling place can become a refuge, your own sacred haven. Your home can become a personal retreat to go to for replenishment, renewal, rest, and relaxation of mind and body; a stable place to recuperate so that you can go out and face the world again, and what's more, you can awaken your home to a vitality and liveliness that will add to your own sense of aliveness.

The difference between these two scenarios is the ingredient called Quintessence, a vital life energy that revivifies the occupants rather than depleting them. We know our bodies are made up of the essential elements, but what animates them? Essence, chi, life force, prana, animating energy, there are many words in many languages to name this essential ingredient—Spirit—the element that brings vitality to inanimate objects, without which the other four are lifeless.

Calling Spirit home is a multidimensional task. Emotionally you determine which of the four archetypal styles resonate with your unique self. Then mentally, physically, and intuitively you set about creating that setting. The missing link that is so often not included when creating our homes is the quintessential, spiritual dimension.

Bringing Life into Your Home

One way of introducing Spirit or life force is to incorporate actual living things in your home, such as plants, flowers, and pets. When a home is made up of entirely inanimate objects, it's bound to feel lifeless. Notice how many photographs in shelter magazines were taken with pets included in the picture. Owning a pet doesn't necessarily mean having a hard-to-care-for animal. Cat owners find caring for these pets easier than most dogs. Even a goldfish can add animation to a lifeless setting, and, as most animal owners will tell you, pets will return your care with unconditional love. Surely that's worth a little extra effort on your part. If you're not a pet lover, or you travel a lot or have no time in your life to devote to a living animal, then perhaps plants will work better for you. Plants are indispensable in recycling dead air and adding vital oxygen to closed spaces. It's essential to keep your plants healthy though, so if you have trouble keeping plants alive, try substituting fresh flowers or displaying bowls of fresh fruits or vegetables. Dying plants, rotten fruit, or stagnant water in flower vases will absolutely negate your well-meaning attempts to introduce vitality. When adding natural ingredients, keeping them healthy and fresh is essential.

A friend's aunt lives in a condominium in San Francisco and works in a rather sterile office building. With no time or place to garden, she treats herself to a large bouquet of fresh flowers every week for both her office and home. What a great way to bring nature indoors and gift yourself as well!

A view of nature from the living areas of your home is another way to bring life inside. Open window coverings to see outside, install a bird feeder close by, and build a window box or fill patio areas with pots of flowers. In a house in the Southwest, we replaced a living room window with French doors and then walled in an adjacent area to create a private courtyard. With a fountain in the middle and colorful flowers that attract hummingbirds and butterflies, nature is literally brought into our home.

My daughter's station in her new hair salon looks out on a small patio. We found a delightful old painted wrought-iron table and chair set, surrounded it with pots of flowering plants and *voila*, as she looks out her window she is able to feel revitalized all day, in spite of her hectic schedule.

Do you have a pet in your home? If so, just for a moment think of the vital life energy that your pet has added. What other ideas can you think of to add living things to your space? What view do you have from your windows? Can you enhance it with flowers or plants?

Include the Occupants' Personalities

Life force is added by including the personality of the occupants. Who are you and what makes you unique? The inscription over the doorway at Delphi, "Know

Thyself," is an important axiom to take into account when creating spiritual space. Know what it is that makes your heart sing and then display your passions in your home. If you love to read, introduce your books as treasured friends; if travel is your passion, objects from special places you've visited should be included among your accessories; if cooking is what brings you joy, then use your cookbooks and favorite utensils as decorative elements. When you are surrounded by things you love, you will respond with joy. Just looking at your favorite things can bring you out of the doldrums.

Many interior designers and parents put the overall coordination of the color scheme and chosen style over the desires of other family members or occupants, and a lot of people are intimidated by interior designers. They give over their power and decision-making options because they either lack the time or quite often the confidence to play a role in designing their own homes. Frequently clients think that the interior designer has the expertise and the good taste and he or she must know more than they about what would be best for them, but if your home does not reflect who you are, it can be the most unsatisfying place to be, no matter how tastefully it is decorated.

A previous client was redecorating her entire house. We were discussing color selections and schemes that we would use throughout. When we got to her teenage daughter's room she told me what she, the parent, had envisioned. "How does your daughter feel about that?" I asked. She said her daughter wanted some horrible teenage thing that wouldn't look right with the rest of the house. I gave her the best advice I could, "Why not allow your daughter to do what she wants to her own room, and simply shut the door?"

In her book *Soul on Fire,* Joan Borysenko describes the following situation she experienced as a young girl. "I arrived in my new room to find a decorator's vision of paradise suited to a New York career woman. Kelly-green custom bedspreads, matching drapes, and sophisticated serigraphs topped off new mahogany furniture. No one had asked my opinion. I hated green, I hated the whole room, and I wasn't allowed to change anything or even to sit on the beds without removing the spreads because it would have spoiled the decor. The bedroom felt like a surrealistic Holiday Inn in which I was to reside as a permanent stranger, forever barred from leaving any sign of my occupancy."[2]

This feeling of alienation, of not belonging, was to stay with Joan for many years. Joan's story underscores the importance of creating a home that reflects who you are. It cannot be taken lightly, for it is psychologically more significant than we have acknowledged in our futile attempts to follow current styles and create chic décors. Remember that what delights your inner essence may not be in style or even considered in good taste, but don't let that dissuade you from surrounding yourself with what you find to be truly beautiful.

Creating spiritual shelter is quite different than just decorating a house. It involves knowing the deep longings and passions of the inhabitants. It requires bringing in positive energy, feelings of safety and well-being, and selecting furnishings and materials that provide not only physical comfort, but also emotional and psychological sustenance. It also requires the active participation of the occupants.

One of the nicest compliments that I receive from clients is how much the newly designed space feels so natural and comfortable; and how much they look forward to being at home. One client recently told me that her friends comment, "Your home looks just like you." I work closely with my clients to understand what colors, patterns, and styles reflect their innermost tastes. I encourage them to bring their own accessories—their unique hobbies and treasures—into their redecorated home and personalize it. Whether you're working with a design professional or doing it yourself, make sure that your individuality and the personalities of the other occupants are expressed in your home.

Whenever you see something that brings you joy, make a note of it. If you see a magazine picture of an interior that takes your breath away, tear it out. Start paying attention to your feelings. When you walk through a furniture store or model home, what styles and patterns catch your eye? Write down your favorite songs and movies. What style of architecture attracts you? What kinds of

patterns please your senses? Make a list of the countries
where you would love to travel. Keep a file or journal of
everything that makes your heart sing.

Creating Sacred Spaces

Another way to bring Spirit into your space is by creating sacred spaces within your home, places where
you keep your spiritual objects or shrines. Small altars
need not be obtrusive but can be something small and
unique, such as a treasured box, beautiful to look at
when closed, in which you keep your personal sacred
amulets, opening it or displaying the contents only
when you choose. Private areas of your home are great
places to create shrines. The top of your bedroom
dresser or a shelf in your bathroom can transform an
unused space into a sacred place. Even an object as
small as a candle in a glass jar with a picture of your
personal sacred deity glued on the front can serve to
create a spiritual atmosphere.

One of my current clients had a wonderful piece of
folk art made for her years ago in Oaxaca, Mexico.
From a chunk of unusually shaped wood and other
found objects, the artisan created a female figure decorated with milagros and pieces of costume jewelry. This
delightful folk art figure now occupies a lighted niche
in the kitchen where she rules as the "Kitchen Goddess." Another personal sacred touch in the same home
is a tile mosaic the owner commissioned from her son's
friend, an emerging young artist. The work, titled "Mary

as a Teenage Mother," is appropriately and proudly displayed on the hearth in the living room; serving both as decorative art and sacred artifact.

Another client's husband is an art collector. Too many similar pieces of sculpture were creating an impersonal feeling when placed strategically around the living area. One day we decided to take a robust female sculpture off her pedestal and place her on an open kitchen shelf. She was instantly transformed into a spiritual being that looked so at home ruling over the kitchen!

In my small home in the Sonoran Desert the whole house is literally a shrine. Specially made niches, walls, areas above the doors, cubbyholes, and shelves are filled with folk art and sacred artifacts. My husband made a recessed shelf between the studs in the kitchen wall, about fourteen inches wide and twenty inches high. Primitive antique doors found in Santa Fe enclose the brightly painted shelves. In it I keep miniature sacred objects, things that have special meaning for me. When I wish to display my personal icons, the doors are open, but when closed it looks like a charming cupboard. An unusually shaped niche in the bathroom houses a stone mother and child (presumably the Virgin Mary) I found in a small shop in Toledo, Spain. In the bedroom another niche was created for a very ancient female figure given to me by my father-in-law from his personal collection of antiques just before he died. Unfortunately, I don't know her age or history, but she is sacred, nonetheless. Above the front door and the kitchen door are folk art angels, guarding and blessing the home. In the living room a shelf is lined with antique *santos* (handmade wooden statues of Catholic saints) and surrounded by *retablos* (metal folk art signs painted in a primitive style, either of a saint or a picture of an event where prayers were answered with a healing). Most guests are not "put off" by the abundance of spiritual artifacts, but find the home comfortable and welcoming, and since the folk art is regional, the style feels at home in this southwestern desert region close to the Mexican border.

Sacred artifacts in our homes become reminders to be thankful for our blessings as well as our lessons. As we pass by a symbolic artifact we can simply touch it, light a candle next to it, or acknowledge in some small way that we honor Spirit. These seemingly small acts bring an attitude of reverence into our home. Instead of cold, dead inanimate enclosures, our homes can come alive. You don't have to fill your home with sacred artifacts as I did in my Southwest abode however, to bring Spirit into your home. As I previously mentioned, private areas make ideal settings for your most intimate icons.

What artifacts do you own that have a sacred aspect? Could something become sacred if it were placed in a special area? Look at your belongings and find those things that have special meaning. Perhaps it's something as ordinary as a small rock you found in a place that felt especially spiritu-

al, it might be a picture of you or your mother as a small child, or a piece of jewelry that belonged to your grandmother. Now find a special shelf or table where you will display the item, maybe even placing a votive candle or vase of flowers next to it. Once you start, you might find that creating sacred spaces within your home can be addicting!

An Attitude of Gratitude

Many people find that thanking Spirit for the abundance in their lives is a magical way of creating a more positive life. When we enumerate all of the things that we have to be thankful for, suddenly the "bad" doesn't seem so overwhelming. Attitude begets gratitude, or perhaps it's that gratitude begets attitude. Either way, changing a negative attitude to a positive one by being grateful for all of our blessings is a simple and effective way of calling Spirit into our lives. Rather than mechanically mentioning the same things each day, try to think of several new things to be grateful for: the wag of a dog's tail, a baby's eyes, the moon shining through a cloudy night, the smell of coffee in the morning, a warm fire in the fireplace on a rainy day, walks in nature when the leaves are changing, fishing in a gurgling stream, and a phone call from a caring friend. How much more meaningful these everyday occurrences would be if we were to show our gratitude to a wonderful universe that loves and supports us rather than dwelling on terrorist activities, the falling stock market, wars and potential new wars, felling of old

growth trees, poking holes in the atmosphere, pollut-
ing the air, pouring toxic wastes into the water and
poisoning the food supplies, and on and on. This is
not to say that we should not be concerned with the
destruction of Mother Earth—quite the opposite. When
we love and treasure our earth abode we will not
mindlessly add to her demolition nor will we be so
complacent when others ask us to agree with their destructive activities. In small ways great wonders are
performed. Each one of us must incorporate within
ourselves a profound love and respect for our earthly
home before we can truly save it.

Inviting Spirit Home

The most obvious way of incorporating the essential
fifth element is to openly invite Spirit to dwell with
you in your home. Inviting sacred ancestors to be part
of your life is not the same as conjuring up ghosts. The
spirits of benevolent ancestors have been called on as
protective deities since time immemorial. Personally
inviting Spirit, guardian angels, Ancient Mother, Father God, sacred ancestors, spirit guides, and teachers
to protect your home and family and share your space
is the quintessential way of bringing Spirit into your
dwelling. This can be done alone and in private or
during a ritual enacted with family and friends. Each
morning a call to Spirit to guard and protect your
home and family offers an inspirational start to your

day. (A specific ritual for Calling in Spirit is offered in chapter 9, Housewarming.)

In contemporary society, one of the most elusive elements in making a nurturing home is this ability to create within it a feeling of reverence or spirituality, or for that matter, the very idea that we should do so. For a home to truly nourish the inhabitants, it must feel alive with the animating essence that invites sanctuary. The soul of the home itself must be encouraged.

Without Spirit in our homes, the lack of awe and mystery is felt in every aspect of our being. When nothing is sacred, nothing seems to support us. We feel we must do everything alone and against all odds. We have no powers to call upon. This belief is a sad commentary on contemporary urban life. When we are separated from our spirituality we tend to see only the problems and the negativity in the world—hope is elusive. If, instead, we incorporate Spirit "down here," right in the midst of our dwellings, we can free ourselves of these limiting beliefs. We can connect on a daily basis with our higher source, and thus empowered can transform our mundane personal environments into sacred sanctuaries that lovingly embrace us.

Start by creating a simple phrase to invite Spirit to dwell with you. Rather than being somewhere in the sky, envision Spirit as part of you and everything that surrounds you. As you begin to bring Spirit into your home, you will feel a vital energy start to inhabit your space. Your home will become your trusted friend and ally.

---

1 Osbon, 184.

2 Joan Borysenko, *Soul on Fire*, New York: Warner Books, Inc.,
  1993.

Chapter 9

Performing

The human psyche apparently loves ritual and is reluctant to live without it.[1]

Barbara Walker

Rituals

Rituals are enacted symbolic ceremonies, performed consciously or even subconsciously. Simple ritualistic acts contain patterns and stories of much greater depth and meaning than is apparent on the surface. Performing rituals focuses our intent, using symbols and body movements, which in turn magnifies the effects. For instance, lighting a candle is a simple act, but behind that act are the power of intention and the magnitude of the universal memory (collective unconscious) that remembers the thousands of years and millions of times when similar rituals have been performed. Your ceremony takes on a more mythic meaning than just physically lighting a candle. The associations with Fire elements are also brought into awareness. Passion, inspiration, and energy fuel our desires and give momentum to our prayers.

With Fire we can put passion and action into our quest or burn away negative thinking that holds us back. When we employ Water elements in ritual, we bring flowing, purifying, cleansing energy to relieve negative emotions and energy. Earth grounds us and brings us fully into our bodies so we can truly feel the sacred moment. Air moves away stale energy, keeping ideas fresh and innovative, and Spirit, the heart of ritual, when called in to guide and protect, adds life force to our dreams and goals. The symbolic enactment of ceremony using some or all of the five elements to symbolize and energize our intentions generates powerful creative forces. The process of creation starts with an idea (Air), then we add emotion (Water), next we physically do our part (Earth), passion and inspiration are ignited (Fire), and with the guidance of Spirit we can accomplish our wildest dreams.

These simple but profound rituals that follow have been practiced in some form for thousands of years. Orthodox Catholic churches still perform rituals involving the four elements: incense (Air), holy water (Water), candles (Fire), and flowers (Earth); vestiges of ancient ceremonies performed in temples and private dwellings to consecrate and purify the space.

The loss of ritual in contemporary society is a significant loss. We can become overwhelmed in our struggle to survive in what we perceive as a dangerous landscape. Without connections to our Higher Power we feel hopelessly alone and abandoned. Re-enacting ritual is a simple but powerful tool for reestablishing connections to our Spiritual Guides.

Following are a number of rituals for use as they are, or personalized to fit your unique needs: rituals for Calling in Spirit, Calling in the Four Elements and Four Directions, Blessing Food, Ridding Negative Energy, Purification Ceremony, Holiday Celebrations, and Housewarming. These are only a few examples of the many rituals you might employ. Feel free to personalize them, adding your own words and ways of doing things. The rote performance of rituals is meaningless—empty words and phrases mean nothing. You must add your energy to the rituals in order to activate them. Since your active participation is essential, it is important that you feel comfortable performing them. Private rituals are very effective and will help you feel more at ease. You won't feel so hesitant to sing, shout, or cry as you might in public. Later, when you are more confident with performing rituals, you can add a few trusted friends or family to your circle. There is synergistic power in numbers.

Calling in Spirit

An initial ritual often performed before other ceremonies is Calling in Spirit. Asking Spirit to be present is paramount to creating positive experiences during the rest of the ceremony, and makes the seemingly mundane more sacred. Whatever words you choose to use for Spirit: Higher Power, Spirit Guides, Guardian Angel, or other specific deities by name, is your prerogative. Asking for the protection and guidance of Spirit lends positive energy to your ritual. This can be done silently as prayer, or chanted and sung aloud. It's important that you feel comfortable. Use a simple phrase such as:

> I invoke the presence of my Spirit Guides, Angels, God, Goddess, All That Is, to be here during the ceremonies today. Protect this space and bless this time to be used for the highest good of all involved.

Calling in the Four Elements and Four Directions

Acknowledging the four elements and directions brings the power of each element into your ceremony. As you face each direction, call in the powers of the elements associated with that cardinal point. Start by calling in the Spirits of the East, Spirits of Air.

> Great Spirit(s) of the East and Air, blow away the debris that clutters my mind and my

thoughts with old and trite ways of thinking.
Help me to fly above my problems and see
them from new perspectives. Give me clarity
of mind to understand the lessons inherent in
my problems.

However you decide to phrase your invocation be
sure to innumerate some of the element's aspects that
you want to call in to support your ceremony. Since Air
represents our mental ideas, this is a perfect place to
begin any new creative endeavor—with your intention.

Turning toward the south, invite the Fire elements
(Odin, Merlin, Magician etc.) to bring their properties
into your ceremony.

Spirit of the South and of Fire, fill me with
passion to create my dreams. Ignite me with
energy and spontaneity. Burn away what is no
longer needed so that I may be free of encum-
brances that hold me back from attaining my
true potential.

Next, turn to the west and invoke the presence of
the Spirits of Water, or name a specific archetype such
as Isis, Venus, or other deity associated with the Water
element. A simple chant might be,

Goddess of the West, Lady of the Lake, etc.,
anoint this ceremony with the purifying and
renewing properties of water. Let my emotions
flow freely without blockages of fear. Fill this
space with love.

Finally turn to the north and invoke the presence of
Mother Earth, Gaia, Hera, Demeter, etc. A sample invocation might be:

> Bless me with your abundance, your fertile and
> protective energies. Ground me that I may be
> truly present during this time. Bring my aware-
> ness into my body that I may participate fully
> in the sensuousness of earth's bounty.

Creating an Altar

In addition to verbally calling in the Spirits, you might
consider setting up an altar for your ceremony. This
will help to create a sanctified space and add to the
mystical significance. Your altar can be a table top or
dresser, a corner of your kitchen counter, a special box
that is used only for sacred rituals; or it can be outside
in nature, under a tree or by a stream, with a distinc-
tive cloth spread on the ground or a circle of rocks in a
wooded area. You may also wish to incorporate a real
object that symbolizes each element during this ritual.
Using a symbolic article is an excellent way to actual-
ize the elements and bring their images into the physical plane rather than just in thought form.

Water can be introduced by filling a special container with purified water. Blessing the water yourself
or asking Spirit to bless it, leaving it outside in the
sunlight and/or moonlight, or boiling away the impu-
rities on the fire can make plain water more sacred.
Maybe you can get water from a well or free-flowing
spring. Adding a few drops of scented oil or dried

herbs or sea salt to the water are also excellent choices for creating "holy water." Other symbols of Water are mirrors, glossy surfaces, shiny objects, blue shimmery fabrics, sea shells, fish- or frog-shaped amulets, and other water-related things.

Earth objects abound: rocks, crystals, fruit, flowers, herbs, salt, or bread, to name just a few. A pinch of sea salt or a crescent-shaped piece of dough placed on the altar can simulate Earth's properties. In ancient ceremonies bread and salt were frequently used to signify the body of Mother Earth.

Fire is typically represented by candles. Smudging the air with scented smoke from incense or lighted bundles of herbs employs both Fire and Air. Other Air artifacts could be angel figures, feathers, bird amulets, and a hand-held fan or a sky-blue altar cloth.

If using symbolic objects, as you face each direction and invoke the presence of the elements, place the object representing those elements in their corresponding directions on your altar or cloth. This is an excellent ritual to use when you set up your household altar.

Blessing Food

In Roman and other ancient homes a sampling of food and drink was always offered to the household spirits before the occupants themselves partook. Breads were given special significance by decorating them or shaping the loaves into symbols of the Great Goddess. The

hearth was often used as an altar, and in Greece and
Rome a shrine to Hestia or Vesta was maintained there.
A bit of food was offered to the fire in her honor. In
eastern Europe salt was tossed into the flames in honor
of the hearth goddess. Reenacting this ritual is a way
of reintroducing ancient ceremonies and continuing
time honored traditions. Also, offering gratitude, as we
previously mentioned, is a way of enumerating our
many blessings and placing our intention on positive
rather than negative images.

If you have a fireplace, before you partake of your
meal take a small morsel of food or salt and toss it into
the fire as you say a prayer of offering to the hearth
deity. In the summertime, whenever you use a bar-
beque, you can do the same thing. If you don't have a
fire, you can hold a small bit of food on a skewer over
a candle flame as a burnt offering.

Ancient customs also included offering a libation of
wine to the household deity before the participants
drank any themselves. Similar to our contemporary
practice of offering a toast, this is a symbolic way of remembering and thanking Mother Nature (or your own
special household spirit) for earth's abundance. A special glass can be set out for the house spirit, either privately in the kitchen or openly at the table. Pour a sip
of wine or other drink into the vessel as you offer
thanks to your own personal deity, guardian angel,
Dionysus, ancient ancestor, etc.

You might wish to incorporate the traditional blessing of food in the form of prayer before eating. Or, if you practice a form of energy work such as reiki, you can place your hands over your food and invoke positive energy. Even without formal attunements, you can perform this ritual by placing your hands over your food and asking for Spirit to bless the food. This simple act brings in higher vibrational energy to our food.

Clearing Negative Energy

Negative energy can accumulate in areas of disuse, areas where angry or violent emotions have been present and areas where the air is stagnant or blocked. Vacation homes, abandoned homes, and places of little use are ripe for stagnant energy buildup. Homes where emotions rage, and anger or violence prevails are also prime targets for negativity. Violent television shows or videos can produce the same harmful energy. Other spaces we might not suspect are cluttered areas, corners, behind furniture, and other hard-to-reach spots where energy gets trapped. Much like pollution in cities, negative energy gets clogged in areas where there is little energy movement. Clearing detrimental energy is an important ritual to perform on a regular basis to prevent a buildup of stale air.

Materials Needed for Clearing
Negative Energy

Choose at least one from each category:

- Air: drum, rattle, bells, or other noise makers, or use your hands to clap the air, or blow air from your mouth (for extremely low, negative vibrational energy, loud noises are more effective).

- Fire: candles in safe containers, incense sticks, or bundles of lighted herbs (use a bowl, large shell, or other safe container for the embers).

- Water: a spray bottle or bowl with holy water (see Calling in the Four Directions for ways of creating holy water).

- Earth: salt is the traditional Earth element used in cleansing ceremonies. Use sea salt or rock salt without added iodine. You may also use a little sea salt in your spray bottle of water to conveniently add Earth's grounding energy, thus combining the two elements for ease of use.

Clearing Negative Energy

When clearing negative energy be sure to start the ceremony by Calling in Spirit. Do not bring fear into the ritual, and keep all activities centered in love. What you think about you draw to you. People who are centered in fear, anger, or violence attract those energies to themselves. When clearing a space where violence has occurred you need to ground yourself and ask Spirit to protect you with a shield of love and light.

Optional: Call in the powers of the Four Elements and Four Directions (see Calling in the Four Elements and Four Directions earlier). All the elements can be called in to move negative or stagnant air. Air keeps energy moving, Fire is purifying, Water is cleansing, and Earth is grounding.

If performing this ritual by yourself, make sure the objects you carry are easily transported, as you will be moving during the ceremony. You might choose to go through the house more than once, using different elements. For example, the first time through you can use noisemakers and chanting, the next time smudging, and then spritzing the air with water and sprinkling with salt.

Start in the center of the space first, clapping, drumming, rattling, or using other noisemakers to start moving stagnant energy (a new broom is suggested in the Housewarming ritual and can be used here also).

Next, smudge the area with smoke, either from a candle, incense, or a bundle of herbs. Move the smoke with your hand, a hand-held fan, or blow it with your breath.

Spritz the air with purified water, or sprinkle it with your fingers or a branch of herbs.

Sprinkle a few grains of salt (salt in the water can substitute), especially in corners and at all openings such as windows, outside doors, and fireplace openings.

Move in a clockwise direction (the right-hand direction sends energy out).

State your intention in a clear and firm voice as you go, "I intend that all negative energy be removed from this space," or, "With these symbols of the four elements I cleanse and purify this space." Use a simple but direct and forceful phrase.

As you spiral through the space, gather the negative energy and take it outside.

When you get to a grounded spot, shake the negative energy out, asking earth to absorb and neutralize the negativity, or move to the farthest edge of your property and state that the stagnant energy is hereby banished from your home. (A ritual for blessing the home and bringing in positive energy is included in the Housewarming ceremony.)

After completion, it is a good idea to shower and remove any negative energy that might have collected on yourself or your clothing. At the very least, drink a glass of water and wash your hands.

Purification Ceremony

Ancient priestesses regularly performed purification rituals, washing and sweeping their temples before and after ceremonies took place. They were well aware of the importance of fresh and clean surroundings in creating sacred space.

Tending your home and keeping it clean is a way of showing your respect for the shelter and love that your home gives you. I'm not talking about compulsive fastidiousness, but frequent cleaning and dusting of furnishings and objects to keep the energy vibrant.

Areas of your home that are filled with clutter attract stagnant energy. Stagnant energy is very similar to dust particles, only not so visible. When air is not moving freely it becomes heavy and filled with physical pollutants as well as unseen emotional and psychic pollutants. Don't let this overwhelm you if you are a collector or pack rat—just chip away at areas that are literally dragging you down. Bit by bit, throw away or recycle all those accumulated things that you haven't used for a while. The result is well worth the effort. When you see the energy in your home vibrating with vitality, it will inspire you to persevere. *Poco a poco se va lejos* is a wonderful Mexican saying meaning "little by little we go far."

As a reiki practitioner, I frequently use reiki to realign and purify the energy in my home. It is a wonderful and loving way to create a positive environment. I also like to do a short purification ceremony each time I clean house. It really makes housework seem more like a holy ritual and takes the drudgery out of it. Playing classical or other inspirational music as I work sets the tone and alters and raises vibrational energies. I often do one room at a time. First I thoroughly vacuum and dust. I use a long-handled feather duster to get cobwebs around the ceiling and light fixtures as well as the lower areas. The feathers are also wonderful Air symbols. Then I light a candle and spritz the air with holy water, directing the water mist toward all corners. I then ask Spirit to bless the space, and leave the candle (either unscented or a good quality aromatherapy one) burning in a safe container for a while afterward. Over the years, I have had many people come to my home after a purification ritual. Unaware that I had performed one, they would often comment on the serene feeling that was present. Before I entertain or have a meeting at my home, I often perform this ceremony; it sets the tone for a peaceful and loving gathering.

Holiday Celebrations

Creating meaningful traditions are excellent ways of forming ties with ancestors and future generations. Many of our contemporary traditions have been commercialized and neutered, leaving them void of significant meaning. Start your own celebrations with symbols and rituals from antiquity—this will add deeper meaning to special occasions. Every culture has time-honored celebrations that can enhance your own connection to ancestors. You can learn about various ethnic traditions by researching your personal heritage and the celebrations they recognized. For instance, if you are of Irish descent, you could create a ceremony during the time of Imbolc (May 1) and introduce some of the ancient traditions surrounding the goddess Brigit. Those of eastern European ancestry could make a "kitchen witch" replicating Baba Yaga. A "corn dolly" made from the last stalks of corn to guard your front door in autumn is an ancient western European tradition, often still practiced during the Thanksgiving holiday in the United States.

The changing of the seasons during the equinox and solstices was honored by many of our European ancestors. The approximate dates of the equinoxes and solstices are: March 21, the Vernal (Spring) Equinox, the time of year when night and day are of equal length; June 21, the Summer Solstice, the day of longest sunlight; September 21, the Autumnal Equinox, like the Spring Equinox, night and day are of equal length; and December 21, the Winter Solstice, the shortest day of the year. You can keep these traditions alive by lighting candles, creating bonfires, planting seeds, or bringing fresh flowers to friends and neighbors.

During our regular recognized holidays you might bring an ancient tradition back. For instance, Halloween was known in pagan Europe as All Hallow's Eve, when the door between the world of the dead and the living opened slightly. Many believed that communication with the deceased was more easily accomplished on this night. What a perfect time to pay our respects to departed loved ones. In many parts of Mexico during *Dia de los Muertos* (Day of the Dead, also known as *Dia de los Santos,* or All Saints Day), families visit the gravesites of their loved ones, bringing food, flowers, and personal items that the deceased person enjoyed. It is not a maudlin time, but a time of honoring the dead by celebrating them. Many towns in Mexico and the southwestern areas of the United States hold parades on this day. Their streets are filled with buckets of fresh flowers, paper flowers, and wonderful Day of the Dead memorabilia, like papier mache skeletons. I certainly feel this is a healthier way of celebrating than children bringing home sacks of candy and worried parents disposing of the contents.

Even though Halloween has been commercialized, it is an American version of All Hallow's Eve. The masks and demons represent our fears of ghosts and goblins and witches. Perhaps by dressing up in costumes representing them, in some way we also celebrate them and lessen our apprehension.

I remember when I was a small child; our local pastor's wife was quite upset that I was dressing as a witch for Halloween. She told my mother it was sacrilegious, and she considered Halloween to be a heathen celebration, and quite possibly it is a vestige of an ancient pagan ceremony. All the more power to it!

Housewarming Celebration

Housewarming is a very ancient tradition celebrated when someone moved into a new home. In Greece and Rome, burning embers were carried from the ancestral home's hearth to the new house, ensuring the continuation of the family and the blessings of the goddess Hestia or Vesta.

Today housewarming celebrations usually center on having a festive gathering with food and drink, foregoing an actual ritual. Traditionally, however, and I agree, it was the ritual portion that was the most important aspect. In creating a housewarming celebration, decide whether you want to do the actual ritual with friends and family, or by yourself first and then invite company to celebrate afterward. If you do include guests in your ritual, make sure they agree to help uphold the sacred significance of the occasion. If you are performing it alone, you may want to combine elements as mentioned in the ritual for Clearing Negative Energy, as you will be moving during the ceremony.

Before beginning, think of several intentions that you have for your new home. How do you wish your new home to function? What aspects of home are most important to you? For example, you might want your home to be a sacred retreat providing renewal and regeneration, or a shelter protecting the inhabitants from outside stress. Or you might want your home to be a reflection of yourself, surrounding you with all the beautiful things you love, becoming a source of unending joy. It might be a place for creating and nurturing a family, etc. Forming your intent for your home is a very important act, and will be brought into the housewarming ritual. Your intention sets the tone and calls in the energy of the home. You attract to you that which you strongly intend. Without your intention, you might be at the mercy of other people's intentions. So take some time and make a list of the important aspects that you wish your home to possess, and how you want it to function. You might even break down each area of the home, listing specific aspects of each room and how you want the room to feel.

Supplies for the Housewarming Ritual

Have at least one item from each category on hand for the ritual.

- Air: hand-held fan, rattle, bell, drum, noise-makers (or use your hands or breath to move the air).

- Fire: candles in safe containers, incense, bundled smudging herbs such as sage or sweet grass (a bowl or other container to catch the burning embers) Note: If it's possible to bring actual or symbolic fire (a candle that was used there) from your previous residence, this is a terrific way of bringing energy and good spirits with you, honoring ancestors and carrying on ancient traditions.

- Water: purified water (may be scented or salted) in a spray bottle or bowl. If you choose a bowl, the water can be sprinkled with your fingertips or a small bundle or branch of fresh herbs like rosemary, lavender, bay, or a sprig of greenery (myrtle was a traditional choice) dipped in the water.

- Earth: salt (sea salt without added iodine).

- Spirit: inspirational music, chanting or clapping.
- A new broom.

The Housewarming Ritual

If you have friends participating, each person can carry an object, but if performing the ritual alone, combine the salt and water and use an incense stick, smudging bundle, or candle in an easily transportable container; use your voice or hands to move the air so you aren't carrying awkward items as you move about. When performing the ritual with guests, give each participant an object to use and briefly explain its use.

Start by calling in Spirit to protect and bless the participants and the home during your ceremony.

Begin in the center of the home, preferably near the fireplace.

Either the owner or the group leader will lead the guests in a single file through the home.

Moving to your right in a clockwise direction (start by removing old energy), the first person uses the new broom to symbolically sweep the area clean (this can be done separately and first if performing the ritual alone). This is a symbolic gesture; you will not be sweeping the entire space.

Move through each room in a spiral clockwise direction. As you go through the house, make sure to move the energy in corners and closets as well.

The next person follows the leader and moves the air with a fan, shakes a rattle, rings a bell, sounds a drum, claps their hands, or blows with their mouth to vibrate and move the stagnant air (if you are performing your ceremony with friends several different objects can be used).

Another participant carries a candle, incense, or smudging bundle, and directs the scented smoke into the recesses of each room, still following in a single file.

The next participant carries the holy water and mists the air or dips their fingers or a wand of rosemary or lavender (myrtle and bay were traditionally used as well) into the water and sprinkles it into the air.

The last person sprinkles a pinch of sea salt in each corner and at all openings, such as windows, fireplace, and thresholds.

Chant out loud a simple phrase as you go such as "Out with the old; in with the new," or "All negative energy, move from this space!"

Continue throughout the house and then to the outside where you will deposit old stagnant energy into the earth for neutralization. If possible go to the outside edge of your property. When you release the energy, use a flicking or shaking movement to indicate that the energy is released here.

The next step is to perambulate the property three times counterclockwise (if it is a free-standing house). In certain countries this was referred to as "beating the bounds." If it is an apartment, condominium, or for other reasons you are unable to walk freely around the property, this step can be done within the home. While you walk the boundary three times, ask Spirit to provide protection for your new home. Salt may also be used during this time to create a circle around your home.

Before re-entering the house by the front door, state your intention for your home, then greet and invite ancestors, household deities, and all harmonious spirits and energies to dwell there.

You might choose to install a symbol or bury an object now near the front door as a protective amulet.

Then circle the interior of the home in a counter-clockwise direction (left hand receives), chanting blessings and bringing positive energy into your new residence. (If you were unable to perambulate the outside of the home, do this step three times.) A great chant is simply the word "Home." When repeatedly chanted this word resonates on a deep level, much like the Eastern mantra OM.

Rather than using loud noisemakers (drums or pots and pans) as we did to banish lower energies, use a chant or bell to resonate with higher vibrational energies during this part of the ceremony.

Finish the ritual with a toast to the new home (be sure and offer a libation to the household guardian) and food for the participants. Bread, fruit, and cheese were often used in this ceremony to represent prosperity for the new home. Include a burnt offering to the hearth goddess, and have fun!

Additional Housewarming Traditions

- If you have a fireplace, lighting a fire with fire from your ancestral home or previous dwelling is a very ancient tradition for bringing the ancestral spirits with you to your new home.

- It was traditionally believed that housewarming celebrations were best done on a waning moon.

- Protective amulets can be hung over doorways or placed beside the fireplace during this celebration.

- Jewish housewarming ceremonies include placing the Mezzuzah over doorways and hanging a Star of David to ward off evil spirits.

- Herbs such as bay, myrtle, rosemary, frankincense, and sandalwood were an important part of ancient housewarming rituals. Any good quality aromatherapy oil can be warmed or added to the holy water, or a bundle of these traditional herbs used for smudging.

- A pot filled with fresh water and herbs slowly steeped on the stove or in a slow cooker will fill the air with purifying aromas. (Be extremely careful that you don't forget them!)

- One very old housewarming recipe calls for rosebuds for love, lavender for preservation, and rosemary for protection, along with salt water for blessing the home.

- A friendly ancestral object (something meaning-ful to you such as an amulet representing your personal connection to Spirit) can be carried during the procession.

- A "luck box" inside the front door was used in some cultures to contain symbols of things that you wanted to bring to your home: a coin signi-fied prosperity, flowers for love, a fruit pit for hospitality, rice for fertility, etc. This small box could also be buried close to the threshold.

- If you choose to keep the "luck box" indoors, a small protective amulet could be buried by the front door instead.

New Home Dedication

If you are building a new home you can follow an ancient tradition by depositing protective elements under the threshold. In many historic rituals, people buried the bones of their deceased ancestors here. You might want to bury a picture or personal article that belonged to a loving grandmother or other ancestor, or an icon representing Ancient Mother such as a bird feather, snake skin, or cowry shell under your new home. Create your new home dedication ceremony by including the rituals for Calling in Spirit and Calling in the Four Elements before you bury your icon. Some people also incorporate a protective incantation into the ceremony such as "May only those who come in love and peace cross this threshold." You may also wish to add any intentions that you have for your new home at this time.

Any occasion can be made more auspicious by adding ritual, and it is fun! Use your imagination and creativity. You'll be surprised how even mundane tasks such as housecleaning can become sacred purification ceremonies using ritual.

---

1 Barbara G. Walker, *Women's Rituals,* New York: HarperCollins Publishers, 1990, 5.

Chapter 10

Propitious Principles

When I create a room in my home, I express
that beauty in the colors I choose and how
I use them. And when I walk through that
room, I feel that I am walking through my
soul.[1]

Marion Woodman

Location, Location, Location!

If you are one of the fortunate who can pick your ideal
site and build your dream home, you could choose the
orientation of the living spaces according to the most
favorable climate conditions and the best views. You
could also take advantage of natural lighting and passive solar heating by noting the direction of major
weather patterns, and locating your sensitive living
spaces—quiet rooms such as bedrooms, and large exposed areas of windows—away from the path of strong

winds and storms. Available views are important con-
siderations—both good and undesirable. Whenever
possible, major living areas should be situated to take
advantage of spectacular vistas, and rooms with small
windows (laundry room, closet areas) assigned to
areas with the least desirable views.

In the Northern Hemisphere a southern exposure
(the rooms with a view, or the largest bank of windows
facing south) is ideal. The sun goes south for the winter, and dips low enough in the southern sky to provide natural lighting through south-facing windows.
In the summer, as it travels north, the overhang of the
roof shades the hottest days of sunlight, making this
orientation a natural heating and cooling factor as
well. Rooms that are used mostly in the daytime, the
kitchen and family rooms for instance, would do well
to have a southern exposure, capturing the maximum
amount of daylight. Artificial lighting is not needed
and the daylit rooms feel inviting. If this is the direction of the best views, you are doubly blessed.

When the sun rises in the morning, the light is soft
and welcoming. Bedrooms, bathrooms, and breakfast
rooms that face east gently wake to the cheerfulness of
morning sunshine. The softer energy of the morning
sun allows you to gradually awake from your dreams
and rise to cleanse and purify in the shower or bath,
and you can slip away for an afternoon nap without
direct sunlight disturbing your respite! In the heat of
the summer, the hot, setting western sun is on the

opposite side of the house. The bedroom is cool by late afternoon, not stuffy or overheated—perfect for sleeping.

Rooms with northern exposure have cool, consistent light all day. Many artists long for studios with north-facing windows, not because the light is warm and welcoming, but because it is a steady light, and the shadows of the subject matter do not vary so much during the daylight hours. Most north-facing rooms need some artificial lighting, even in the daytime. The formal living room and dining room used more often in the evening or for special occasions or a home office where computer screens function better without direct glare, are best located here.

West-facing rooms receive the late afternoon sun, making them suitable for family gathering and play areas, creative/hobby rooms, or activity areas such as laundry rooms.

Although most of us are not able to situate our homes in the most desirable location, or lay out the placement of the rooms as we might wish, we can compensate for less-than-perfect circumstances by using color and lighting to enhance the atmosphere within each room.

Take a few minutes to assess the layout of your home. If you are considering building a new home, you might wish to include some of these ideas in your plans.

Lighting

Whenever possible, natural lighting is the ideal way to bring light into your home. Since this is not always possible, even in the daytime, artificial lighting is a necessary adjunct. If you're like most of us, and own or rent an existing home that is not ideally situated to gather natural light, there are several things you can do that will compensate for less-than-perfect natural conditions.

For years architects and interior designers believed that man could create a more perfect interior environment than nature. Buildings were planned with uniform fluorescent lighting, no shadows, no variations, just full, complete light all day. We now find that this steady monotonous fluorescent lighting is unnatural and in many cases unnecessary. In countless situations the environments were overlit. Too much light was used when it wasn't needed, creating a wasteful use of electricity. The constant, steady unchanging light was tiring, and the hum and buzz of the ballasts were irritating. Now, buildings are being planned to make use of natural daylight, a light that is friendly and pleasing, supplemented with lighting that is closer to the task. To provide all of the lighting from the ceiling is wasteful when less wattage is needed as the light source is located closer to the job being performed. Some areas where no tasks are performed are in shadow, both conserving energy and creating a more interesting ambience. Lighting on dimmers allows for variations of intensity for different purposes. A light over the dining table can be dimmed and candles used to set a mood, or intensified if the dining table is being used for task purposes such as homework.

Fluorescent or Incandescent

Warm, incandescent light offers inviting, pleasing light, but sometimes brings with it unwanted heat, especially in summertime or in locations that have warmer year-round temperatures. Fluorescent light is traditionally thought of as a cool source of light, enhancing cool colors in a room and neutralizing or graying down warm colors, and creating unflattering skin tones. Although improvements have been made to correct some of these negative qualities, I am not a great advocate of fluorescent lighting, except in certain situations where energy efficiency is critical. For example, in large kitchens in warm climates when enough incandescent lighting is required to be functional, it can also create too much heat and become a real energy gobbler. Fluorescent lighting is the least expensive and most efficient energy source; however, I still think fluorescent lighting is unnatural and uninviting and I avoid using it as much as possible, except where indicated by building codes. (In California, building codes for new construction require the use of fluorescent lighting in kitchens and baths to reduce energy usage.) In general, I prefer to use less artificial light throughout, except in task areas, where I bring the light source as close to the task as possible. Skylights are a great way to bring in more natural lighting and reduce energy costs.

Areas of light and shadow create interest and mystery. Lights from different heights in a room add another dimension to the overall effect. Uplighting under indoor trees and plants or sculpture can create intriguing patterns on walls and ceilings. Spots of light directed at artwork provide dramatic focal points. Lighting a pathway down a hall could be done with wall sconces rather than all overhead light. Lamps are great accessories as well as good sources of light. Again, if you use a variety of lighting sources and dimmers to vary the intensity, you are able to create change that follows nature's lead. Nature's light is ever changing. Early morning light is slightly warm and gentle, noonday (high task time) more direct and stronger, in the afternoons the shadows start to stretch, and evening brings warm, radiant sunsets and the cool twilight before the moon and stars bring out the twinkling night lights. On some days the sun is behind clouds, either all day or playing hide and seek as the clouds dart across its face. The moon, of course, varies continually, ever waxing and waning. Seasons also bring a variety of light sources, bright reflections of snow from a more distant sun in winter; warm, long shadows of light in autumn, clear and crisp primal light of springtime, and the searing white sun of summer. I suggest that you vary the source, color, placement, and amount of your lighting to focus on beauty and sustain the shadows for added mystery and drama.

Candlelight and firelight remind us of our ancient roots. The movement of flames creates patterns that dance across the walls and ceilings, animating the room and inviting magic and mystery into our homes. Light is such an important factor that it can literally transform the whole nature of a room without changing anything else.

Are you satisfied with the lighting in your home? Is there sufficient light to perform tasks such as reading? Do some rooms have too much overhead lighting and not enough mood lighting? Changing the lighting in your home does not have to include costly electrical work. Dimmers are easy to install, and portable lamps with three-way bulbs can provide a variety of light intensities. What other ideas can you think of to incorporate mysterious, magical qualities with light?

The Energy of Color

Your home is filled with visual cues that subconsciously feed you information. If that information is from negative sources you can, without realizing, create an environment that is depressing and damaging to your physical and psychological well-being. Color is an important environmental element that needs to be understood and used wisely, because color is light and light is energy. When you paint your walls a certain color you are creating energy that affects you on many different levels.

You don't actually see colored objects, but rather, the rods and cones in the retina of your eyes respond to electromagnetic waves of energy; the visible portion is the color spectrum of light. Color is the way you see light reflected by an object. You respond to colors physically, emotionally, psychologically, and culturally. Color affects you on an energetic level. Studies have shown that blood pressure and heart rate can be raised or lowered when a person is exposed to certain colors; and colors are used to heal certain physical disorders. Jaundice is treated with violet light, for instance. Ancient people, including Pythagoras and the Egyptians, used colors for healing. They believed that different colors affected different parts of the body. Today researchers in a field of study called chromotherapy are studying the affects of color for treatment of disease.

Culturally, colors are associated with different customs and ceremonies. In the Western world white is a sign of purity or innocence, ceremonially associated with weddings and bridal gowns; red is flashy, stimulating and has historical references to "red-light districts," adding sexual connotations. In Asian countries red is symbolic of good luck, and white, used as a color for mourning, signifies death. Our response to color is shrouded in cultural connotations.

Color trends are introduced in fashion and furnishings according to social and economic situations. In the United States there is a national color council made up of people from various industries that decide what colors will be popular for the coming season. The colors popular today will be outmoded in a few years. Some of your dislike or prejudice for certain colors may have to do with those colors being out of style. For example, you might have an aversion to a certain shade of green because it reminds you of 1970s appliances. Another color might bring back memories of your grandmother's sofa, and depending upon your relationship with her it could be a good or bad memory. There are no bad colors per se, only those you associate with negative experiences. You might have an aversion to black, reminding you of funeral clothing, witches, Dracula, or the villain dressed in black, but once it was a revered color associated with the fertility of Mother Earth.

Just as there are no inherently bad or unlucky colors, neither are colors lucky or good, but the use of color can be either harmful or beneficial. Since you are constantly surrounded with colors, and you have the ability to control the colors in your personal environment, you can use color to your advantage, and choose those that will have the affect you desire. When you wake up to a day filled with sunshine and flowers you feel delighted, on other days you might wake up to an overcast day where everything takes on a somber gray appearance that can depress your mood as well. The colors you choose for your home are just as influential on your spirits as the weather.

Warm and Cool Colors

Since you are affected by color on all levels, it is important to explore the effects of various colors when used in your built environment. In general, we divide colors into two groups: warm and cool. Warm hues are orange, red, and yellow; cool hues are blue and most purples. Green can be either warm (more yellow) or cool (more blue), and is considered a balanced color widely seen in nature. Purple is also a combination of warm (red) and cool (blue) hues. Magenta is a warm purple (more red than blue) and lavender or violet are cool hues (more blue than red). Warm colors are considered active, arousing, and cheerful. Cool colors are passive, restful, and somber. Emotionally, people feel more peaceful in cool-colored rooms and more stimulated in rooms of warm colors. Ideally, you will want to combine warm and cool colors in your home, using relaxing colors in rooms where you want to unwind and exciting colors in areas where creative stimulation is desired.

Psychologically, a room painted orange or red makes us think the temperature is warmer than it actually is. We also tend to see walls painted with strong, warm hues closer to us than those with cool pale colors. This phenomenon has to do with the way colors appear in nature. When you look across a wide expanse of land-scape with mountains in the distance, the colors close to you appear warmer and clearer than those on the far horizon. In design we use this principle to make small rooms appear larger or large rooms more intimate.

Are you naturally drawn to warm or cool colors? How does this correspond to your own temperament? Are you cool and aloof or warm and friendly? Do you surround yourself with colors that compensate for imbalances in your personality? Do you enjoy mixing colors from both warm and cool families in the same room? Take a few min-utes and analyze the temperature of colors toward which you are drawn.

Intensity

The intensity of a color also has a lot to do with the way it affects us. Intensity is the amount of strength or clarity (saturation) of a color. When a color is less intense, it means the color is grayed down, or more neutral. Strong, clear red is intense, brownish red is less intense. Clear, deep blue is intense; gray-blue is less intense. The majority of colors in nature are less intense with small accents of more intense colors. For example, the less intense browns and greens of na-ture's background are enlivened with accents of in-tensely colored flowers. You can take cues from nature in your own home, using less intense colors for the larger areas such as walls and floors, and more intense colors for accents in smaller areas: pillows, chair fabrics, and accessories.

Tints and Shades

Colors are also greatly changed by adding white or black. When we add white the resulting color is called a tint or pastel—when black is added it is called a shade. Tints are more feminine and shades are more masculine.

Are you drawn to lighter pastels or deeper shades? Which is more predominant in your home?

Complementary Colors

Another thing to know when using color is that color is greatly affected by its surroundings. A color can appear stronger when used near a color that is its complement. When colors are arranged on a color wheel, colors that are opposite each other are called complements. Blue and orange, red and green, yellow and violet are complements. If you were to paint one wall an intense red and then put a green chair in front of it, both colors would appear stronger and you might even have trouble looking at them for any length of time. A physical reaction takes place that makes the colors vibrate—the strength of the two energies appear to fight each other.

Complementary colors can also neutralize each other when mixed together as in paints, or when threads of complementary colors are used together. A woven fabric of red and green yarns will appear brown from a distance, yellow and violet will look gray. Whatever colors already exist or are reflected through your windows will affect the appearance of the color. When you understand that color is the energy of light, you will realize that what looked perfect in the paint store will appear entirely different in your home. I always recommend buying a quart of paint and trying it in your setting to see how it looks. Even then, we can be shocked when we see it intensify on a large wall. In general, select paint colors for walls that are less intense than you want the wall to appear when painted.

Color and Lighting

Another very important factor when selecting color is lighting. Daylight versus artificial light, and incandescent versus fluorescent, all make tremendous differences in the way colors appear. Look at the color sample during daylight and the way natural lighting comes into the room and also under the artificial light at night. The direction of each wall and the way light reflects off the wall will also change the color's appearance, so paint a sample on each wall to see the various affects. The color that looks so vibrant in natural daylight might look dead under artificial light. In general, incandescent lighting enhances warm colors and fluorescent lighting grays them down. Cool colors respond just the opposite.

Have you ever painted a room in the daytime, only to be quite shocked by its changed appearance in artificial light at night?

Color and the Elements

Water, Earth, Fire, and Air are each associated with their own distinct color palettes. Fire and Earth are aligned with warmer colors, Water and Air with cooler colors. Fire's colors are the warmest and Water's colors are the coolest. Earth's colors are generally warm, but include a variety of greens that can serve to balance the temperature. Air's cool hues include deep saturated tones of purple. Water and Earth, the two feminine elements, generally have lighter colors than Fire and Air, whose hues are darker.

By now, you've probably decided whether you are an intellectual Zeus, a dreamy, romantic Aphrodite, the practical, earthy Hera, or the magically, creative Merlin. When working with one elemental style, the colors are predominantly warm or cool, depending upon which one you choose, but no matter what your dominant style, you can choose warmer or cooler colors to incorporate into appropriate areas of your home.

Water's cool, pale blue, aqua, and lavender are perfect colors for bedrooms and bathrooms—areas where you wish to unwind and relax. If you want a lighter palette, use off-whites with slight lavender or blue undertones. Then for balance, spring colors such as light yellow and clear pink are great adjuncts.

Earth's balanced, slightly warm palette is ideal for kitchens and family rooms. Food is more appetizing and spirits more energized with earth's color scheme. Since it is a balanced scheme, you are not promoting hyperactivity or an eat-and-run atmosphere with a too-warm color group. Typical earth colors incorporate a variety of greens, plus off-white, beige, brown, and terra cotta as background with splashes of bright hues as accents; a perfect variety for balancing warm and cool colors throughout the home.

Fire's colors are dark and warm and generally less saturated than Air's rich, dark, cool colors. Its hues include deep gold, reds, rusts, warm greens, and various shades of orange and warm brown. These colors are the most active and passionate, making them ideal for creative work areas.

Air's cool hues align with mental activities. Cool white and gray are the neutral tones; accents include black, deep blue, and purple. Warmer purples such as magenta are used to balance a too cool and stark atmosphere.

When we use one major element as a theme or we combine two elements that are closely related, we can incorporate aspects of the other elements for balance. Each element's color scheme has a predominance of either warm or cool hues, but within those hues there are tints and shades that can be warmed or cooled to create the perfect atmosphere for the function of the room. You can also combine the color scheme of one element with hues from an adjacent element's pallet or a spark of contrasting color from the opposite element. For example, let's say your major element is Water. We now know that the cool blues are perfect for bedrooms and baths, so you have a large variety of shades to choose from in those rooms. Water is also associated with cool pale greens and whites that team up nicely with a touch of apricot or peach (Earth) for a great color scheme for kitchens and family rooms. For more active rooms you might use predominantly apricot, with accents of terra cotta and blue or green. Offices and other places where mental activities take place are ideally painted in cool white, light blue, or blue gray. Your whole color scheme is still predominantly Water, but variety has been added to create balance.

If Fire is your chosen element, the warm colors of this palette are perfect in the kitchen, family room, and other active areas. Cooler greens and blues can be incorporated in the bedroom and bath for more relaxing pursuits.

Another example is the cool Air palette of colors. Stark metallic finishes and a predominance of black and other dark hues can feel very sinister if not balanced with touches of bright, vibrant color such as clear red or magenta, especially in less formal, more active areas of the home.

Unless you have a strong support group, you're probably wearing the crown of Arthur at work, the gown of Venus at night, the work gloves of Demeter in the garden, and the hat of Merlin in the hobby room. Integrating all the various aspects of yourself is wholesome. Your home can reflect this multifaceted persona. The kitchen can be more earthy, the bedroom and baths more romantic, the office clean lined and uncluttered, and the studio or hobby areas more creative.

When our homes are either all cool or all warm, they feel imbalanced. Take your cues from nature's ever-changing but always harmonious use of color. If you use predominantly cool tones with accents of warmer hues in one room and reverse the proportions in another room, you will be able to adjust the colors according to the function and lighting needs of each room. You can also make your home more versatile during the year by using slipcovers, a variety of throw pillows, and area rugs to change the color schemes with the seasons.

Are you ready for some fun? Painting a room is one of the least expensive ways to create a drastic change in your environment. Try experimenting by painting a hallway or entryway (there's not so much furniture to move) with a fun and lively color from your chosen element and see how it makes you feel. Look at your existing color scheme. Is it predominantly cool or are the colors mostly warm? What archetypal style most appeals to you? If you aren't currently using colors from the style that you are most drawn to, can you find any areas where you can use those colors, perhaps as contrasts?

Space Planning

An important aspect of creating a healthy habitat is the free flow of energy throughout the home. We talked about regularly clearing blocked energy and cleaning out clutter in chapter 9. The way we arrange furniture within our home is vital to the free flow of energy, both physical and psychological. Allow at least a three-foot-wide path for major walkways in the house and a minimum of one and a half to two feet for accessing lesser-used areas. When you have to step around objects you psychologically feel obstructed on your path. Poor furniture layouts or layered clutter might photograph well for a magazine layout, but are not healthy for everyday living. When you can't get around something easily, neither can air nor energy circulate freely. Don't crowd your coffee table next to your sofa or you will literally feel trapped when you are in the middle and someone sits next to you. It's true that some people enjoy more things in their environment—Earth is a more cluttered style, for instance—but narrow walkways, stacks of books on the floor, items piled on the stairway, or just neglected cleanup will cause you to feel mentally and emotionally blocked. A really powerful piece of advice is to clean up your clutter and clear up your stumbling blocks. Removing obstacles that prevent you from freely moving around your home will allow you to move through other areas of your life with more ease.

When my sister read about clearing out clutter from her home in a preview chapter of the book, she put it down with dismay. She told me she had never been a tidy housekeeper and if that was one of the requirements of a spiritually nurturing home, she was never going to attain it. Don't feel overwhelmed by the suggestion to reduce clutter or equate that with having to create an impeccably clean house. However, if your home is littered with stacks of paperwork, unopened mail, and things that have not been filed or put away, you might want to really think about what the clutter in your home symbolizes. Do you feel that life is so cluttered with constant demands for your time and attention that you can't see a way out? If so, try reducing the clutter in your home a little bit at a time and see if you notice a difference in your ability to accomplish things in other areas of your life that you didn't think possible.

Furniture that sits at an angle and blocks corners of the room can also contribute to blocked energy flow. If you do have furniture placed diagonally across a corner in your room, make sure you move it out and clean behind it frequently. This is a common place for negative energy to build up.

How does the layout of your furniture allow for ease of movement through your home? Do you see any areas of blocked energy? Try rearranging furnishings that feel too congested. Put away unnecessary materials that clog the free flow of energy, then begin to notice how much freer and more creative you feel in all your endeavors.

Creating a Focal Point

Psychologically, it's important to have a view of something beautiful as you work or sit and relax. The placement of fixtures and furniture should take into account views from windows and doors as well as interior views. If your home overlooks the ocean or stream or a beautiful meadow and your furniture backs up to the windows, you have literally turned your back on nature. Most executives know that the office with a window and a view is prime property. The low person on the team gets a cubicle with no view at all. If your home has a view, arrange your furniture to take advantage of it, and make the most of rooms with good natural lighting by using comfortable chairs and convenient side tables that invite you to sit down and read, or just enjoy the scenery.

When you are fortunate enough to have a lovely fireplace, make sure your seating is arranged to fully appreciate the fire and its ancient symbolism. If a room lacks a view or an interesting architectural detail, use artwork or unusual accessories or furniture as the focal point, and be sure to select your art according to your passionate feelings about the work rather than merely matching the décor.

In each room there should be something really beautiful that catches your eye, but if there are too many things vying for your attention you can become overwhelmed. Prune out your collections. If you own several collections, display them at various times rather than all at once. This balance of enough but not too much will vary with individual tastes; just remember that nature does not have a fabulous sunset all day long, or we would be tired of it by nightfall.

Walk through your home and see if you can find the focal point in each room. Are there rooms without one and others with too many? How can you arrange your furnishings to be more favorably aligned with excellent views?

A Sacred Space

Have at least one area in your home that is your own personal sacred space. Whether it is an entire room, or just a chair and end table, is not as important as the act of setting aside. According to mythologist Joseph Campbell, ". . . those who seek to achieve fully the goal of life should set aside a sacred space."[1] How fortunate if it can be your entire home! If not, even a small, quiet corner is sufficient. A place that houses and protects your sacred icons and offers something beautiful to look at is ideal. This simple space can become a treasured friend who opens her arms when you need respite.

Can you think of a special place within your home to make your own sacred space? Why not create one now— after all there is literally no time but the present.

---

1 Osbon, 252.

Chapter 11

Auspicious Symbols

It has always been the prime function of
mythology and rite to supply the symbols that
carry the human spirit forward . . .[1]

Joseph Campbell

Home as the Impetus for Change

As you begin to implement some of the ideas suggested so far, you will find that your home can become the impetus for dramatic change in your life. You can create an environment that will encourage the birthing of your deepest desires. Colors, textures, patterns, light, and symbols all act as subliminal messages. Whether you are aware of it or not, you are deeply affected by the environment in your home. You can consciously utilize positive symbolic images that support your physical, emotional, and spiritual needs. Your home not only provides shelter from inclement weather, a safe place to store and prepare your food, protection for children and elders, but also a supportive environment where you can learn and grow and become self-actualized.

Creating with the Four Elements

Whenever you create something, whether it is a cake or a piece of art, you go through four steps of the creative process. First you have the idea; then you ruminate for a while, conjuring up more details, seeing the finished product in your imagination; next you gather together the supplies and ingredients you physically need to bring your ideas into reality; and finally you arrive at the actual, creative, alchemical aspect of mixing together all the various parts into a magical finished product. Before you consciously begin any creative act, call in Spirit, either in ritual or by simple intention, and set the scene for a more flowing, harmonious process.

These steps are symbolized by the four elements, plus the quintessential fifth element:

- Air represents your thoughts and intentions—your original ideas.

- Water symbolizes the emotions that you attach to your thoughts. It also represents the dream time or period of incubation when your thoughts are empowered with greater significance.

- Earth is the power of Now; of being fully present with your five senses—not thinking, thinking and more thinking, but giving your mind a rest as another aspect of the creative process is activated. It is also the phase of creation that calls for physical doing: actually going out and getting the ball rolling by taking the necessary physical steps of buying supplies, filing a business license, or setting up a studio, etc.

- Fire is the inspirational insight, the creativity and passion, the impetus that drives you to transform your initial idea into creation.

- Spirit is the Muse: the creative guiding source. Call in Spirit in whatever form you feel comfortable during any creative process. This most important step plugs you in to a connection with the cosmic creative force.

Air

When you are too attached to one element, you can get lost in that one aspect of the creative cycle. When you are only in the thinking stage (Air) you can be filled with wonderful ideas that don't go anywhere. Lost in your thoughts you might think things like, "If only I would have done something with that idea I had. I could have really made a fortune, but now someone else has done it and I'm missing out." Or, "My mother (father, teacher, etc.) told me my ideas were silly, so I'm not going to do anything with these ideas. After all they really are just nonsense." Or, "If I just stay in my mind, dreaming of new ideas and inventions, I won't really have to go out and actually create anything. I can be safe here in my mind and make believe anything I want." Maybe you stay stuck with trying to solve unsolvable mysteries in your mind, or you have the same conversations with people over and over again, or you might be the kind of person who is always coming up with great ideas that soon fizzle out and go no further. Many professors are stuck in the thinking stage of creation, knowing all about something, but not really able to go any further than just thinking about it over and over, from every possible angle. Sometimes this type of person is part of a team of specialists—the "think tank" or "ideas" person that comes up with new ideas, and then other support personnel implement them.

Water

When you get bogged down in the Water phase you wrap too much emotion around your thoughts. The emotion that holds you back from creating your dreams is almost always based on fear. Intuitively you might know something, but when you begin to wrap negative emotion around it, it starts to look like this: "I feel very strongly that the idea I had for a new venture is right for me, but what if I use all my money to start it with and it doesn't work. Then I'm looking at not being able to pay my rent, make my car payment, buy food etc., etc." So you don't do anything. Fear has you paralyzed, stuck in the emotional stage. You may feel a deep excitement when you think of designing your home—then the fear emerges, telling you that you can't really make it happen for one reason or another.

Earth

Earth aspects are centered in the here and now, your physical body and environment. When you are reminded to be in the Now, it means to get out of your mind and your negative emotions, to stop and smell the roses, to be fully present with what is in your current physical presence, not in the past and not in the future—those areas that paralyze us. When you are performing simple tasks and your mind is not wandering to what needs to be done next, but is focused in the physical, you transform mundane duties into "holy acts." So many of us fail to really live in the Now. For so long we have been stuck in the mind or the negative emotion of fear, that to actually ground ourselves in the physical is a very novel thing to do. Mindfully performing each task as you do it rather than thinking of what you will do next or what you forgot to do earlier is a very essential act of creation that many of us are failing to do. There is great wisdom in this, especially when you are also balanced with other areas of creativity. Consciously working in the garden or cooking and taking care of the house, lovingly feeding your plants and animals are all significant tasks. You stop and breathe and feel and smell and hear and see, really see what is all around you, but there is another aspect of the physical where you can get mired down. Do you sometimes feel you have too many pressing physical needs and that you don't seem to have time to do the creative things that your heart cries out to do? "I wish I could paint, write, create a new endeavor, etc., but I have to take the kids to soccer, serve on the school fund-raising committee, pick up the dry-cleaning, go to the grocery store, mail a gift to my mother . . ." (you fill in the blanks). You can get so caught up in the everyday physical world that you forget to dream; or maybe you perform all your physical tasks without being aware that you are doing them because you are lost in your head. Nothing is really meaningful; everything is mixed together, thinking, dreaming, doing, one big overcooked soup with no distinct flavor. When you work harmoniously with the Earth phase of creativity, you perform each task with your complete attention. You will be surprised at how much you can accomplish, and how much fun you will have doing what you once thought of as drudgery. This is the time to ground your thinking process. You might have a great idea and be very emotional about it, but unless you take the actual steps of physically walking this idea into reality: filing the proper paper work, finding the best location, hiring personnel, setting up bank accounts, doing the actual physical tasks that need to be done to create your dreams, they will eventually stagnate.

Fire

Fire represents the transformation of ideas into reality. This is the process of creativity itself: painting or creating original artwork, designing a beautiful new kitchen, writing inspirational poetry, or any other creative endeavor that has been brewing in your thoughts and dreams that are now physically transformed into being. To get trapped in this phase is to start mass producing your artwork, or rubber stamping your design ideas, or writing lackluster poetry. You are caught up in the creative phase without the required new ideas, incubation, or groundedness that it takes to create original works of art. Many great creators went through the original process step by step and then created a masterpiece, only to be discovered and asked to reproduce it over and over again. Something is lost when this happens; whatever you have created has now lost its Spirit, its quintessential essence. You know when you are creating vital projects just as you know when you are just going through the motions without any true inspiration. When all aspects of creativity have been included in your creative endeavor the end results will feel unsullied and vital.

Sometimes, in the midst of creating, I lose my inspiration. If I'm writing I can no longer think of one more thing to say or if I'm designing a space for a client I can't come up with one new novel solution. I then know it is time to stop trying to wring myself out like a dry rag, and leave whatever I'm doing and go back to another stage in the creative process. I might take a walk in nature, or lie down and take a short nap, but somehow I need to pull other elements into my process. I find that if I stop doing what I'm doing and let other elements enter in, I become re-inspired.

The next time you feel stuck in the creative process, see if you can determine what phase has you bogged down. Then go back and bring other elements into your process. Do you need to let your mind rest for a while and allow new creative ideas to incubate? Perhaps you need to center yourself in your physical surroundings. Stop, take a time out and do something different. Sit quietly and let your Muse whisper in your ear.

The Power of Symbols

Symbols are concise pictorial shapes or marks that can represent volumes of information; able to be viewed quickly, but contemplated for longer periods of time. We respond to them on all levels: physical, emotional, mental, and spiritual. In our home environment we are surrounded by them, but are often unaware of their more subtle, arcane messages. Symbols can be used to offer cryptic information to a few enlightened people without blatantly proclaiming their meaning. We can use them to consciously prompt us to stay centered and mindful as we perform mundane tasks. They can be used in the creative process when we feel stuck by reminding us of areas we tend to neglect. They subtly encourage us to speak our minds and clearly state our intentions, to feel deeply and passionately, and to create whatever we most desire. Symbols have various connotations and can mean different things to different people, but many symbols associated with the home have a common origin, making their ancient message almost universal.

Sacred Symbols in Arts and Crafts

Sacred symbols have been utilized by indigenous cultures in their arts and crafts for thousands of years; Native American baskets and blankets, Turkish and Persian rugs, Pacific Island textiles, African crafts, Celtic designs. In fact, if you study the primitive art of most countries, you will find striking similarities in motifs. Perhaps you are already surrounded by these sacred symbols and haven't noticed them as such. Be cognizant of your surroundings and what messages you are subliminally sending and receiving.

Symbols were used prodigiously throughout times of oppression to express sacred devotion without garnering others' suspicions and potential condemnation. By painting a border of wavy lines and triangular motifs around a room you might signify your desire for fertility—either abundant or reproductive—without proclaiming your intention to the world.

What symbols do you want to incorporate as symbolic of home? A perfect place to start is with your sacred space or altar box, by decorating it with symbols either hand painted, stenciled, or covered with pictures, or three-dimensional amulets. Once you begin you will find it enjoyable to incorporate many meaningful symbols in your home. Pattern designs that relate to ancient symbols imbue the article with cryptic meaning—commonplace, inanimate objects can be transformed into spiritual artifacts.

Activating the Power of the Elements Using Symbols

Each element is associated with a number of identifying attributes. When we condense these properties into a symbol or symbolic object, we incorporate all of the information we know (consciously and subconsciously) about that element into a graphic reminder. It's like tying a string around our finger. We are reminded of a whole story in just one picture or icon. This becomes a powerful tool for creating emotional fulfillment, abundance, passion, and mental clarity, all the things represented by the four elements plus spiritual oneness. As many motivational speakers and psychologists will tell you, what you think about all day you become. If you think about what you lack, you add to the force behind your thoughts to create your reality—more lack. If instead you are reminded of love and abundance when you see a symbol or object, and you surround yourself with those objects, it just makes common sense to understand that you will begin to think in more positive, life-enhancing ways. Magically, the things that you wish to call into your life will appear.

Activating Air Symbols

Since the element of Air is associated with the mental plane and the thinking temperament, it represents our ideas and abstract thought, laws, principles, and morals. Air people are lofty and idealistic, prone to philosophize. The Tarot symbol is the sword. Many wars are fought over morals and idealistic principles—Air also represents the warrior. When you need to stand up for yourself and find your authentic voice, Air symbols can be very useful. The sword and zigzag are symbols historically aligned with the sky gods, as are vertical lines and shapes similar to the Tau cross. A more contemporary archetype for Air is Zorro, who slashes a *Z* with his sword; both the Z (zig-zag) and the sword are prominent Air symbols.

Straight vertical lines represent the male phallic symbol; zigzags symbolize the force of lightning and thunderbolts. Eagles and hawks are large, powerful birds that represent Air in the animal world. Feathers, hand-held fans, bells, and rattles move and vibrate air waves to physically activate this element.

If you are preparing to take an exam, give a speech, or use your mental faculties to your best advantage, use Air symbols for subliminal reminders. Slipping a feather in your pocket, wearing a stick pin on your jacket, or using a pointer during your speech can be powerful subliminal reminders of Air's agile qualities.

Use Air symbols when you need to call in the warrior archetype. Maybe you need to speak to your boss about a sensitive issue that will require gathering up all your courage, or you want to draw your boundaries when someone is trying to invade your personal space. There are times when you need power and strength to face difficult issues, when you need to battle the dark forces, or stand up for yourself—times when you can use a powerful ally. These are perfect occasions for calling in the power of Air. Obelisks, letter openers, a Tarot card with a sword, or other sword-like symbols can remind you of the strong power and courage that you can call on when needed.

Your office or study is an excellent place for painting vertical stripes on the wall, or using a vertical-striped wall covering. Mental stagnation is a common occurrence especially, if we sit at a computer or in a stuffy room for long periods, trying to read or write. Opening a window will circulate the Air and give the necessary freshness to stale thoughts. Air attributes are attracted to clean, uncluttered surfaces and cool, calm colors. If the area where you need to think or study is filled with distractions, you will find yourself jumping up to do other things. If you are constantly distracted, try painting the room where you study a cool color; then clean off and dust cluttered surfaces and reduce your accessories to a minimum. Use one symbol of air, perhaps an angel figure, a bird amulet, or a beautiful feather as your Muse, rather than lots of little objects. The quill used by our ancestors as a writing implement is a beautiful symbol of mental acuity.

With an overabundance of Air energy we feel much like an absent-minded professor, detached from our bodies, floating in space. If your temperament is such that you stay in your head most of the time, try using more Earth archetypes to ground yourself. A picture of nature, a rock, or vase of flowers on your desk can remind you to keep yourself balanced and your feet firmly planted on the ground.

Another way to compensate for too much mental activity is to take frequent breaks and have a drink of water or walk around a bit, especially if you can get out in nature.

Activating Water Symbols

Water is closely aligned with emotions, dreams, and our love life. It is purifying, cleansing, and free flowing. Water is soothing and washes away negative debris. It represents rebirth, new beginnings, and the freshness of springtime. Its most ancient association is the primeval waters of life, the earliest matrix of life forms. The suit of cups, in the Tarot deck, represents this element. Anything relating to romantic, emotional, or intuitive matters falls under the realms of Water.

Symbols associated with Water are water birds, water snakes, fish, frogs, shells, and flowers found in wet places like water lilies and bog orchids. Wave patterns, smooth glossy textures, sea glass, sea weeds, mermaids, white foam, sounds of waves crashing on the shore, or water tumbling over rocks all remind us of this element.

Whether you wish to attract a new relationship, or entice more romance into an existing one, Water symbols are useful. A bowl of holy water, a glass heart, mermaid, or shell can be placed on your altar space as a symbolic icon; or for more extended emotional issues you can use a stylized wavy line around your bedroom as a border or buy a set of water-colored sheets to cover you as you sleep and dream. By surrounding yourself with Water's colors, materials, and symbols you are reminding yourself on all levels to relax and rejuvenate and let your emotions flow gently; to allow yourself to love and be loved. This will create symbolic cues that can open the door to deep emotional fulfillment.

A small indoor fountain, light blue or lavender accent pillows, or a sensuous shimmery shawl tossed over the sofa or bed invoke Water elements. The Tarot symbol is cups; using bowls filled with lavender as room fresheners repeats both its symbolic shape and color. If your office needs the purifying element of Water, put a clear vase filled with fresh water and irises or hyacinths on your desk to elicit this purifying element.

Too much Water results in a world of fantasy and make believe. If you belong to the category of Dreamer, those who are not in touch with reality but always dreaming of a utopia where Prince Charming is waiting to rescue them, then you need to balance Water elements in your home. Earth elements are grounding and call us back to the physical where we are firmly entrenched in the here and now. Salt, rock, fruit, and other Earth symbols can be used to counterbalance too much Water.

Activating Earth Symbols

In the Tarot deck, Earth is symbolized by the pentacle—the auspicious five-pointed star surrounded by a circle—the ancient symbol of "Happy Homecoming." Earth represents abundance on the material level; issues surrounding our physical well being, finances, and careers. Earth elements help us feel grounded, completely in our bodies using the gifts of our five senses. When we are aligned with Earth energies we are truly in the moment: smelling, tasting, seeing, hearing, and touching. We are alive in the joyful experience of the abundant and loving universe that supports us. He or she "is the salt of the earth" is a phrase that describes a solid, dependable Earth personality.

Insecurity, lack, career questions, or feelings of being spacey and ungrounded are signals that we need to call on Earth's resources. We can do this by displaying symbols of flowers, fruits, herbs, seeds, rocks, salt, food, crystals, gems, or coins—items that represent abundance and stability. Subconsciously we will begin to feel more nurtured. For more long-term support, decorate your home with earth colors and patterns. Paint your kitchen lettuce-leaf green, add floral pillows to your room's décor, hang pictures of flowers or abundant landscapes, and replace cold drab materials with colorful slipcovers. Uncover windows behind heavy draperies, add warm lighting, use aromatherapy oils, play music with sounds from nature, buy a healthy new indoor plant, then nurture yourself with home-made soup.

One who has an overabundance of Earth traits might exhibit stubbornness, and be unwilling to change with a "stuck in the mud" attitude. "I'll believe it when I see it," or "Show me" are mantras of strong Earth people. They may need to have a fire lit under them, or spend more time in the exciting world of possibilities. Fire and Water symbols can remind Earth people to loosen up and expand their beliefs.

Activating Fire Symbols

We know that Fire represents passion and inspiration—your creative side. Active, spirited, productive, assertive, enthusiastic, and stimulating are traits of Fire. Are you burnt out, feeling lifeless and uninspired, dragging yourself through the day with no goals or ambition? Maybe you need Fire's stimulation. Red is the color to do it with. Red represents energy, life blood, passion, and appetite.

People who are depressed or listless can incorporate red, orange, gold, and warm greens into their color scheme, and replace cool fluorescent lighting with warmer incandescent lamps for amazing results. Lighting is very important in this scenario. Many people think that if they paint their walls white and have well-lit fluorescent lighting they are making their homes bright and cheerful. Not so! If a room has dingy reflected natural light, a cool northern exposure or fluorescent lighting as the main source, white walls will look dull and depressingly gray. Instead try a paint color like soft golden beige or pale terra cotta, add warm-colored fabrics on upholstered furniture, use wood instead of glass or metal tables, throw a plush-textured lap quilt over the sofa, lay thick area rugs on hard-surface flooring, and start a fire in the fireplace, if you have one. For a temporary lift, candles are the easiest and most available Fire symbols to use. Other Fire associations are the legendary phoenix, salamander, Vesta, Hestia, or Brigit, the hearth goddesses, magicians and wizards, and their symbols.

In the Tarot, Fire is symbolized by wands. Wands represent our ability to say "abracadabra" and have our thoughts and dreams magically become reality. A Fire personality is action oriented. If you're a dreamer or an inventive thinker whose ideas never materialize, you might add a little fire to your environment and see what happens.

Opposites Attract

When deciding on which symbols to use as the dominant ones in your home, first determine which element makes you feel the most comfortable. Often it is not the same as our personality. We might be hotheaded and explosive and need a cool, calm atmosphere to soothe our fiery disposition. Whenever we have a strong need to balance our personality, we could incorporate into our home more elements with opposite character- istics—those that we lack. For example, if we have a slow, methodical, depressed personality, we may bene- fit by incorporating more Fire symbols. In this situa- tion, stimulating colors and warm lighting can perform magic. When deciding which elements to focus on in your home, take into account those traits that you wish to correct. You might find yourself drawn to your op- posite element just as you would with an opposite personality. For instance, the shy wallflower is often at- tracted to the extroverted, flamboyant character. Your private space is the perfect place to use lighting, colors, materials, and symbols to augment and balance your own personal needs. Some attempts have been made by health-care professionals to create supportive envi- ronments for people with extreme disorders such as mental illness and clinical depression, but more work needs to be done in these areas.

If your overall personality is fairly balanced and you are able to function effectively in all areas, combining elemental styles into more blended or eclectic design schemes will probably appeal to you. Then, whenever a temporary situation arises when you need the help of one particular element, creating a ritual and adding a symbol to your altar is very effective. For the ritual, you can simply state in clear emphatic language what your intention is, then place the symbol on the altar, calling in the help of Spirit or your household deity to activate it. This is powerfully creative!

Home is a Living Entity

Your home is a living entity. We now know, thanks to research in quantum physics, that all matter, animate and inanimate, is made up of tiny particles of light moving in waves of energy. On a subatomic level our bodies are made of the same minute packets of light energy as the coffee table—the only difference is that the energy of our bodies is vibrating at a higher rate. We are constantly interacting on a subatomic level with all matter. You are literally mingling with everything in your home. For instance, when you walk into your house and smell an odor, you are breathing in minute particles (off-gassing) of the materials in your environment. Those fumes are then taken into your body and incorporated in your cellular structure. This is just one tiny example of your total interaction with the environment. You are literally breathing in and breathing out all of creation.

According to poet Diane Osbon, "The people of Findhorn, Scotland, believe that the consciousness of trees goes *beyond the sawmill*, that they are aware of the homes into which they are made and the people they shelter . . ."[2]

We often buy into the belief that everything must be scientifically proven to be valid, but in doing so, we sever the connection to our own intuition. Alienated from our own inner guidance, we cut ourselves off from the sacred source of personal power. Activating the power of Spirit in our homes is a powerful way to re-connect to this intuitive way of knowing.

Sacred Anatomy of Home

In many of our homes, the sacred symbols represent-ing the opening to the womb: Delta (triangular pedi-ment over the door), Omega (arched opening), and Pi (two vertical pillars covered by a lintel),[3] are still there after thousands of years of concentrated effort to erad-icate them. Imagine! The ancient shapes that marked the entrance to the birthing chamber of the Great Goddess are with us yet.

Finding and using symbols of the body of the First Mother as tools for remembering our spiritual connec-tions are more prevalent than you might imagine. When used in simplified form they become arcane messages for our own personal use. We don't need permission to use a triangle for example, but we might have objections from other family members if we were to display statues of various gods and goddesses in our living room. As we mentioned previously, this symbol for the pubic triangle is one of the earliest sacred sym-bols. Along with the number three (also an auspicious

Fibonacci number) the triangle in some form is found on many household objects. It might be a three-lobed flower, or three leaves, or perhaps two triangles joined at the apex forming the ancient symbol for bees, butterflies, the double axe, and the female torso. Connected Vs form a horizontal zigzag pattern found on ancient pottery, and still used on many contemporary artifacts. You can easily incorporate the triangle in your home by using a triangular configuration in arranging three items on a table, such as three candles, or three pillows on the sofa. You might even select wallcoverings or fabrics with small triangular patterns. Triangles connected at their bases form a simplified diamond shape representing, among other things, the vulva.[4]

Circles and spirals are also associated with the body of the Ancient Mother. A circle with a dot in the center can represent the womb and navel, breast, or early round house with fire in the middle. Spirals might represent snakes or the umbilical cord, the connective link with our original source.

In medieval Ireland, the Sheila-na-gig, a stout, odd-looking female protectress, held open her vulva as a charm to counteract death by displaying the powers of life. We don't need to be that explicit! We can use almond shapes, cowry shells, ovals, apples cut lengthwise, figs, peach seeds, an eye, or a mouth to represent the shape of the vulva of the Great Mother. The letters *A, U, V, X,* and *Y* are all symbols of the crotch or entrance into the womb of creation. Horns, crescent moons, snakes, birds, butterflies, and three-petaled flowers all represent the reproductive qualities of our first ancestor. Over the years the original meaning of these symbols has been deemed obscene. It is time we reversed this unhealthy belief!

Have you incorporated a symbol by the entrance to your home to remind you that you are entering sacred space? If not, why not take a few minutes and do so now.

Male Deities

There are hundreds of symbolic associations of ancient deities—both male and female. The sun is the most recognized symbol of the male sky gods such as Ra, Zeus, Thor, and Apollo. Sky gods are also associated with symbols of thunderbolts, hammers, and swords. Oak trees were sacred to Thor, Balder, Jupiter, and the Druids. The legend is told of Thor finding protection under an oak during a thunderstorm. Acorns became a symbol of the protection of oak trees. They were used as amulets to protect against lightning strikes; placed on window ledges or used as pulls on window blinds. Iron, wheels, bulls, crosses, and eagles are all powerful amulets associated with male deities. If you are drawn to an image of a male deity or need to call in these warrior powers when facing your "dragons," there are many to choose from. Male symbols can also be used to help manifest your dreams into physical reality.

Choosing a Household Deity

You may wish to select one personally meaningful icon to represent your own household god or goddess. It can be a statue, picture, or a symbol of your personal spirit guide, a favorite mythological character or animal, or it might be an ancestor, perhaps a grandmother or more ancient relative. Take some time to think of the archetype that "speaks to you," then keep your eyes open for just the right object to appear.

My own house goddess came to me in a wonderfully symbolic way a few years ago. I had enrolled in a shamanic workshop in San Francisco facilitated by the renowned teacher, Michael Harner. In the workshop, we were taught how to "journey" into the realms of the "other-worlds." During one of the exercises, a spirit guide appeared to me first in the form of a bird and then as an ancient goddess. It was a moving experience, and very personal. When I returned home to the city where I lived at that time, my husband said he had a gift for me. Then he handed me a small, antique, stained-glass window showing a robust naked woman with bird wings instead of arms. I was astonished and absolutely thrilled. Of course he had no idea what had happened during the weekend seminar, it was pure synchronicity! He then gave me another surprise; there were two of them, exactly alike. They are my twin house goddesses. One of them hangs in the window of my kitchen in our mountain cabin and the other is with me here in the desert where we spend our winters.

I have numerous other house deities that rule over specific rooms as well. In fact, once you begin to look for a house deity, the right one will seem to just walk up to you and place itself in your hands. Then others will begin to appear in mysterious ways. As if by magic, the perfect ones for you will manifest.

Do you own an icon that would serve as a house deity? If not, pay attention to symbolic references that you encounter. Whenever an object or symbol attracts your attention beyond normal curiosity, your subconscious may be sending you a message. It's fun to find artifacts that represent our private, sacred selves. But watch out, it can be habit forming!

1 Joseph Campbell, *The Hero with a Thousand Faces*, Princeton, NJ: Princeton University Press, 1968, 11.

2 Osbon, 11.

3 Erick Neumann, *The Great Mother; An Analysis of the Archetype,* Princeton, NJ: Princeton University Press, 1991 ed., 158.

4 Walker, *Woman's Dictionary*, 50.

Chapter 12

The Enchanted Dwelling

When the trees were enchanted
There was hope for the Trees."[1]
Cad Goddeu, The Battle of the Trees

The Enchanted Dwelling

An enchanted dwelling conjures images of magic and casting spells; of marking boundaries with sacred circles, using amulets as talismans, performing rituals, lighting candles during ceremonies; of devising herbal concoctions and burning incense to move negative energy. The word enchant is synonymous with delight, and enchanting with charming and attractive, but to be an enchantress is to be a seductress or a witch. Hmmm. Your home can be absolutely enchanting, but not enchanted. I, for one, think it is due time we set about designing our homes in enchanting ways to make them charmingly enchanted! When we do,

our homes will take on magical qualities of mythic sacred dwellings where dreams are realized—islands of
enchantment in the midst of storms and chaos.

Hallowed Ground

The most important thing we can do to create an enchanted atmosphere in our homes is to remember that
the home in its most ancient aspect is considered sacred space, symbolic of the body and womb of the
original Mother. This analogy of oneness with our
Mother's body formed the earliest spiritual beliefs.
Before our own birth, we were indeed one with our
mother—she housed, nourished, and protected us in
her womb, and her blood flowed through our veins.
We were physically connected to her body by the umbilical cord that fed us from her own nutrients. Our
ancestors knew the similarities between our home in
the body of our biological mother and our home in
the body of Earth Mother. They both provide shelter,
nourishment, and protection. Nothing about the female reproductive organs and genitals were thought of
as obscene; quite the contrary, they were considered
sacred. The body of our mother was seen as a micro-
cosm of the greater body of our Earth Mother. As we
were protected and nourished in our mother's womb,
so we are protected in the greater world around us. As
we were one with our physical mother, so we are one
with earth! The idea of separation came much later.

When you enter your home you are entering hallowed ground, and if you are really in touch with this concept, you will begin to treat your home with new respect. You will understand that your home deserves the reverence and love that you would give to any other sacred site. As you might reverently and quietly light a candle in an historic mission, you do the same in your own home. Placing flowers on the coffee table is no less a spiritual act than adorning an altar in the little stone church on the corner. Cleaning your home is the same spiritual practice as scrubbing the tiles of a monastery or washing the marble floors of Vesta's temple. Using cryptic symbols and amulets are just as powerful in your personal dwelling as they were when painted on the walls of gothic cathedrals, surrounding your home's portals with guardian deities no less important than the stone gargoyles carved around the entrance to Romanesque churches. Sitting in quiet meditation in your favorite chair takes on the same lofty meaning as it would on a vortex in Sedona.

How much differently you feel toward your home when you bring sacredness into everyday life. Each act you perform becomes shrouded in mystical meaning. There are no mundane duties when you acknowledge the profound nature of your dwelling. Previous chores become spiritual practices. Aware that you are symbolically tending the body of your sacred Mother—a practice so ancient that it preceded all temple and church rituals of the same nature—you understand

an(   )reciate the importance of creating a
pea(   )ng atmosphere in the hallowed place
whe(   )support and sustenance, spiritually
as (   )ally. Your home will become your
s(   )n personal refuge. It is just waiting
(   )your magical, transformational abilities. With your
intention you can create a healthy, rejuvenating and
vibrant life space—a true enchanted home.

If your home is a rented apartment or mobile home
or even a corner in a room, the bleakest place can be
transformed with reverence. Love and appreciate the
shelter you now have. Our ancestors lived in caves,
and treated them as the most sacred spaces. Rather
than waiting until you can afford to build or buy your
own home, use your imagination and creativity to
transform your current abode, however humble, into a
living shrine. Light a candle or say a prayer in gratitude
as you thank the universe for providing shelter. Send
love to the thousands of people without homes as you
are reminded of the words, "I used to feel sorry for myself because I had no shoes, until I met a man who had
no feet."

Look around at your home; identify the images of
Spirit that surround you. Welcome them and honor
them. Your home is so much more than a place to
hang your hat. It is literally the self-made chrysalis for
your emerging sacred self.

Place pictures or representations of your own personal protective deities, your household guardians, on

your altar or fireplace mantle. Acknowledge their importance and offer gratitude for daily blessings and manifested intentions. Sprinkle salt on the fire and pour a libation in their honor. Mist the air with scented holy water, light candles, and burn incense. Perform a housewarming ritual. Hang protective amulets over the doors, and on the hearth or above the kitchen stove. Fill vases with flowers and bowls with fruit. Use symbolic sacred patterns on textiles and wall coverings. Surround yourself with visual reminders that your home is hallowed space, and that you live in an abundant universe where you are truly loved and protected. The results will be profound!

Think of a few small things you can do today to honor your home. Keep your eyes open in your travels or daily life for objects that represent sacred aspects of your dwelling. Acknowledge your home when you return by greeting it or performing a simple ritual such as spritzing the air with holy water or lighting a stick of incense. Find a household guardian that speaks to you and put it in a place of honor. As you pass by, gently rub your fingers over it, sending and receiving love.

Safe Refuge in Times of Stress

Many of us have experienced periods of deep emotional trauma, times when we felt scraped raw by life's lessons; exposed to our very core. There is no better place than home to find safe, supportive refuge during those periods of excessive stress. Our homes are private and familiar and contain those things that give us comfort: family, pets, and sacred artifacts. When I personally went through my own dark night of the soul, my home and my sacred spaces within became all the more meaningful. I felt a deep peace knowing that at any time I could light a candle or perform a ritual or ask my personal spiritual guides to comfort me. There was no need to find a church that was open where I felt comfortable praying; when I needed respite, my home was my chapel, and, it was already prepared and waiting to serve my deepest needs. Many times, I found peace within the walls of my quiet sanctuary and I gave thanks for my home and the amazing solace it offered me.

There is no more opportune time than the present to create a personal spiritual retreat, available if and when taxing circumstances occur. For most of us, periods of upheaval come in intervals like waves and stormy weather. During the peaceful interlude, we would do well to get our house in order.

In this time of global warfare, falling stock markets, corporate scandals, mass unemployment, and violent weather patterns, more than ever before we long for a safe haven where we feel comforted and nurtured; a place to instill character in ourselves and our family; a place of encouragement and self-empowerment. As you connect with your most ancient ancestral heritage, you can truly make your home an enchanted sanctuary; a wondrous, conducive environment for transformation as safe and nurturing as your mother's womb—a protective cocoon for your own rebirth.

---

1 Robert Graves, *The White Goddess,* Farrar, Straus and Giroux, 1948.

Bibliography

Barrett, Clive. *The Egyptian Gods and Goddesses*. London: Diamond Books, 1996.

Borysenko, Joan. *Soul on Fire*. New York: Warner Books, Inc., 1993.

Campbell, Joseph. *Hero With a Thousand Faces*. Princeton, NJ: Princeton University Press, 1968 ed.

Cooper, J. C. *An Illustrated Encyclopedia of Traditional Symbols*. London: Thames and Hudson, 1978.

D'Aulaire, Ingri, and Edgar Darin. *Norse Gods and Giants*. New York: Doubleday and Co., 1967.

Davidson, H. R. Ellis. *Myths and Symbols in Pagan Europe; Early Scandinavian and Celtic Religions*. Syracuse, New York: Syracuse University Press, 1988.

De Lys, Claudis. *A Treasury of American Superstitions*. New York: Philosophical Library Inc., 1948.

Ellis, Peter Berresford. *The Druids*. Grand Rapids, MI: William B. Eerdmans Publishing Co., 1994.

Gadon, Elinor W. *The Once and Future Goddess*. New York: HarperCollins Publishers Inc., 1989.

Gimbutas, Marija. *The Language of the Goddess*. New York: HarperCollins Publishers Inc., 1991.

Graves, Robert. *The White Goddess*. New York, Farrar, Straus and Giroux, 1948, 1982.

Hoddard, Ian. Catalhoyuk Excavations, http://catal.arch.cam.ac.uk/catal/catal.html

Ions, Veronica. *Egyptian Mythology*. London: The Hamlyn Publishing Group, 1968.

Koch, Rudolph. *The Book of Signs*. New York: Dover Publications, Inc., 1955.

Larousse. *Larousse Encyclopedia of Mythology*. New York: Barnes and Noble Books, 1994.

Macrone, Michael. *By Jove! Brush Up Your Mythology*. New York: HarperCollins Publishers, Inc., 1992.

Metzner, Ralph. *The Well of Remembrance*. Boston and London: Shambhala, 1994.

Muten, Burleigh. *Return of the Great Goddess*. New York: Stewart, Tabori and Chang, 1994, 1997.

Neumann, Erick. *The Great Mother; An Analysis of the Archetype*. Princeton, NJ: Princeton University Press, 1955, 1983, 1991.

Osbon, Diane K. *Reflections on the Art of Living; A Joseph Campbell Companion*. New York: HarperCollins Publishers, 1991.

Opsopaus, John. The Ancient Greek Esoteric Doctrine of the Elements, http://www.notaccess.com/RELATIONSHIPS/ GeometryAl.htm, 1998.

Pickering, David. *Cassell Dictionary of Superstitions*. London: Cassell Wellington House, 1995.

Shepherd, Sandy. *Myths and Legends from Around the World*. New York: Simon and Schuster, 1994.

Spretnak, Charlene. *Lost Goddesses of Early Greece*. Boston: Beacon Press, 1978.

Stone, Merlin. *Ancient Mirrors of Womanhood*. Boston: Beacon Press, 1979, 1990.

———. *When God was a Woman*. Orlando, FL: Harcourt Brace and Co., 1976.

Thorsson, Edred. *Northern Magic; Mysteries of the Norse, Germans and English*. St. Paul, MN: Llewellyn Worldwide, Ltd., 1993.

Waldherr, Kris. *The Book of Goddesses*. Hillsboro, OR: Beyond Words Publishing, 1995.

Walker, Barbara. *The Women's Encyclopedia of Myths and Secrets*. New York: HarperCollins Publishers, Inc., 1983.

———. *The Woman's Dictionary of Symbols and Sacred Objects*. New York: Harper & Row, Publishers, Inc. 1988.

———. *Women's Rituals; A Sourcebook*. New York: HarperCollins Publishers, 1990.

Suggested Reading

Women and Mythology

Eisler, Riane. *The Chalice and the Blade*. New York: Harper-Collins Publishers, Inc., 1987.

Gadon, Elinor. *The Once and Future Goddess*. New York: HarperCollins Publishers, Inc., 1989.

Gimbutas, Marija. *The Language of the Goddess*. New York: HarperCollins Publishers, Inc., 1991.

Reis, Patricia. *Through the Goddess*. New York: Continuum Publishing Co., 1991.

Spretnak, Charlene. *Lost Goddesses of Early Greece*. Boston: Beacon Press, 1978.

Stone, Merlin. *Ancient Mirrors of Womanhood*. Boston: Beacon Press, 1990 ed.

————. *When God Was a Woman*. Orlando, FL: Harcourt Brace and Co., 1976.

Walker, Barbara G. *The Woman's Dictionary of Symbols and Sacred Objects*. New York: HarperCollins Publishers, Inc., 1988.

————. *The Women's Encyclopedia of Myths and Secrets*. New York: HarperCollins Publishers, Inc. 1983.

Northern European Mythology

Davidson, H. R. Ellis. *Myths and Symbols in Pagan Europe; Early Scandinavian and Celtic Religions*. Syracuse, NY: Syracuse University Press, 1988.

Ellis, Peter Berresford. *The Druids*. Grand Rapids, MI:
   William B. Eerdmans Publishing Co., 1994.

Markale, Jean. *Merlin, Priest of Nature*. Rochester, VT: Inner
   Traditions International, 1995.

Matthews, Caitlin and John. *Encyclopedia of Celtic Wisdom;
   A Celtic Shaman's Sourcebook*. Rockport, MA: Element
   Books Inc., 1994.

Metzner, Ralph. *The Well of Remembrance*. Boston and London: Shambhala, 1994.

Interior Environments

Venolia, Carol. *Healing Environments*. Berkeley, CA: Celestial
   Arts, 1988.

Rituals

Henes, Donna. *Celestially Auspicious Occasions; Seasons, Cycles and Celebrations*. New York: Perigee Books, 1996.

Linn, Denise. *Sacred Space*. New York: Ballantine Books,
   1995.

Walker, Barbara G. *Women's Rituals; A Sourcebook*. New
   York: HarperCollins Publishers, 1990.

Index

Acca Larentia (Lara), 45

Aesirs, 38

Air, 24, 61, 86–90, 92–94,
  96, 99–100, 105–106,
  111,114–116, 121,
  124– 127, 129–130,
  132, 136, 138–140,
  143, 145, 154, 158,
  160–161, 163, 165–
  167, 169–170, 174–
  176, 178, 194–196,
  198, 204–205, 213–
  215, 231

Alexander the Great, 40

All Hallows Eve, 171–172

All seeing eye, 80–82

Alpha, 69

Altar, 25–26, 33, 35, 44,
  70, 78, 162–164, 211,
  216, 220–221, 229, 231

Ambulatories, 67

Amulet, 24, 71, 77, 177,
  179, 214

Aphrodite, 105, 108, 116,
  194

Apollo, 40, 224

Aquarius, 89, 121

Archetypes, 8, 13, 88,

108–109, 116, 118,
  120–121, 127–129, 215

Aries, 88, 120

Aristotle, 86

Ark, 26–27

Arts and Crafts, 112, 121,
  211

Asherah, 74

Ashtoreth, 52

Aspelenie, 48

Athena, 39, 58, 109, 116

Baba Yaga, 48, 170

Balance, 64, 92–93, 98,
  104–106, 123, 131–
  132, 135, 139, 141,
  194–196, 201, 216, 220

Balder, 224

Bes, 43

Bird, 29–31, 76, 138, 146,
  163, 179, 214, 225

Bogies, 57

Brigit (Brigid, Brigantia,
  Bride), 25, 29, 47, 52,
  78, 170, 219

Brownies, 54, 56

Butterfly, 30–31

Caca, 44

Caduceus, 49

Cancer, 88, 107, 116

Capricorn, 88, 118

Cardea, 72

Carna, 72

Catalhoyuk, 37, 45–46, 50, 79

Celtic, 5, 45, 47–48, 51–52, 54–56, 63, 79, 211

Chrysalis, 230

Clockwise, 68, 73, 97, 168, 175

Clovis, 7

Clubs, 89, 113, 120

Complementary colors, 192

Corn dolly, 170

Counter clockwise (widdershins),

Cowry shells, 46, 223

Crescent moon, 5, 7, 26–27, 39, 54, 70, 76

Crete, 40

Crone, 33, 47, 88

Cronus, 39

Cross, 73–75, 88, 93, 98, 121, 123, 180, 213

Cups, 89, 107, 116, 134, 215–216

Deae Matres, 47

Delphi, 22, 40, 93, 107, 146

Delta, 69, 222

Demeter, 31, 88, 95, 110, 118, 162, 196

Devera, 139

Dia de los Muertos, 171

Dia de los Santos, 171

Diamonds, 89, 111, 118

Diana, 26, 52

Disir, 38, 77

Dom, 55

Domania, 56

Domovikha, 56

Domovoi, 55–56

Dove, 5

Druid, 112

Duende, 57

Earth, 15, 22, 30, 32–33, 36–37, 39, 58, 61, 64, 73–75, 78, 86–90, 92–96, 100, 105–106, 109, 111–112, 116, 118, 123–129, 131, 133–134, 136–138, 140, 154, 158, 162–164, 166–168, 174, 176, 189, 194–196, 198, 205, 207–208, 215–218, 228

Egyptian ankh, 74

Electromagnetic, 188

Elves, 54–56

Empedocles, 85

Emperor Constantine, 52

Epona, 48

Equilibrium, 64, 92, 103–104, 106, 130

Equinox, 171

Esprit follet, 57

Esse, 86
Ether, 86
Etruscan, 44–45
Europa, 39
Eurhythmy, 99–100, 104
Evil eye, 40, 60, 80–82
Eye beads, 81–82

Fairies, 29, 54–57
Feng Shui, 3, 17
Fibonacci numbers, 97–98
Fire, 25–26, 43, 47–49,
    53, 64, 70, 78–79,
    86–89, 91–94, 96, 100,
    105–106, 112, 120,
    123–133, 135–136,
    140, 148, 153, 156,
    158, 161–164, 166–
    167, 174, 178, 194–
    196, 200, 205, 209,
    218–220, 223, 231
First Mother, 22, 222
Fish, 33, 79–80, 118, 215
Fleur de lis, 53
Flowers, 5–6, 12–13, 32,
    44, 53, 76, 79–80, 95,
    102, 109, 111, 119,
    124–126, 132–133,
    135–136, 138, 145–
    146, 153, 158, 163,
    171–172, 179, 189,
    191, 215, 217, 224,
    229, 231
Fluorescent, 184–185, 193,
    218–219
Focal point, 132, 200–201

Freya (Frigg, Frigga),
Frogs, 32, 79–80, 215

Gabija, 48
Gaea, 39, 53, 88, 109, 118
Gargoyles, 229
Gefjon, 47
Gemini, 89, 121
Genialis, 45
Genii loci, 15, 45, 63
Genius, 38, 45
Giza, 95
Gnomes, 54
Goddess of Laussel, 22, 26,
    68
Golden ratio, 96–97
Golden rectangle, 97–98
Golden section, 97–98
Great Gate, 71
Great Mother, 22–23, 33,
    43, 67, 71, 85, 223, 226
Greek Revival, 69
Gremlins, 57
Guardian angel, 57, 160,
    164

Halloween, 171–172
Haltia, 48
Hamingja, 77–78
Harmony, 91, 99, 101,
    104, 140
Hathor, 43
Hearts, 14, 76, 89, 107,
    116
Hebe, 47
Hecate, 47, 88

Hera, 31, 39, 47, 88, 109, 118, 162, 194
Hermes, 112, 120
Hestia, 25, 43–44, 47, 70, 78, 164, 172, 219
Heverei (witchcraft), 76
Hex signs, 75–76
Hobgoblins, 56
Horn of plenty (cornu-copia), 26–27, 47–49, 88, 110, 119
Horseshoe, 6–7, 24, 69, 71–72, 76–77
Horus, 81
Hourglass, 30
Housewarming, 25, 155, 157, 159, 161, 163, 165, 167–169, 171–175, 177–179, 231
Hygeia, 95, 98

Inanna, 5
Icon, 7, 75, 79, 95, 179, 212, 216, 225–226
Imbolc, 29, 170
Incandescent, 185, 193, 218
Intensity, 185–186, 191
Io, 39
Irrational numbers, 97
Isis, 41–42, 52–53, 105, 109, 116, 161

Janus (Ianus), 72
Jove, 34, 38, 114, 121
Jung, 89

Juno, 38, 45, 47, 109, 118
Jupiter, 38, 114, 121, 224
Juventas, 47

Kikimora, 29, 56
King Arthur, 114, 121
Kitchen witch, 48, 170
Kobolds, 55
Kore (Ceres), 75, 95

Lady of the Lake, 105, 108, 116, 161
Lar, 44–45, 77
Lararium, 17, 77
Larentalia, 45
Le Corbusier, 96, 114
Leo, 89, 120
Leonardo da Vinci, 96
Libra, 89, 121
Lightning, 37–38, 64, 114, 123, 130, 213, 224
Lilies, 5, 53, 79, 118, 215
Lima, 72
Limentinum, 72

Maat, 5, 80
Madder Akka, 48
Magician, 106, 112–113, 120, 128–129, 161
Maiden, 33, 47–48, 87–88
Malergabiae, 48
Mano fico, 81
Mary, 5, 7, 52–54, 151
Matrilineal, 36–37
Medusa, 81
Merlin, 34, 54, 75, 112,

120, 161, 194, 197
Mermaid, 118, 216
Minerva (Merarva), 47
Minoan, 80
Moon Goddess, 39
Mother, 8, 22–26, 31–34,
     36, 39–40, 43, 45, 47,
     49, 52–53, 57, 61, 67,
     69, 71, 78, 85, 87–88,
     95, 106, 109–110, 118,
     128, 151, 153–154,
     162–164, 172, 179,
     189, 205, 208, 222–
     223, 226, 228–229, 233
Mount Parnassus, 40
Mu, 30
Muse, 205, 210, 214
Mut, 39
Mycenea, 69

Nautilus, 97
Nebula, 97
Negative energy, 71, 159,
     165–166, 168, 173,
     176, 199, 227
Nekheb, 29
Nekhebet, 29, 41
Niss (nisse), 57
Norns, 47

Obelisk, 123
Odin, 75, 81, 112, 120,
     161
OM, 69, 177
Omega, 24, 53, 69, 71,
     222

Orchids, 215
Original Mother, 36, 228

Parthenon, 52, 95, 97
Patriarchal, 28, 37–38,
     63–64
Penates, 44
Pentacle, 217
Pentagram, 75–76, 93–96,
     98–99
Pentalpha, 98
Penus, 44
Persephone, 88
Phallic symbol, 40, 213
Phyllotaxis, 97
Piet Mondrian, 96
Pisces, 88, 107, 116
Pixies, 56–57
Pomegranate, 5, 58
Priestess, 105–108, 116,
     127–128
Princess, 105, 108, 116
Puck, 57
Purification, 64, 109, 159,
     168–170, 180
Pythagoras, 95, 188

Quantum mechanics, 36
Quantum physics, 36, 221
Queen Olympias, 40
Quinta, 86
Quintessence, 86, 93,
     143–144

Ra, 38–39, 80, 224
Reiki, 165, 169

Retablos, 152

Rhea, 39

Rituals, 3, 8, 15, 17–18,
   25, 32, 53, 60–61, 63,
   139, 157–159, 162,
   168, 170, 178–180,
   227, 229

Robin Goodfellow, 57

Romanesque, 229

Rosmurta, 49

Saga, 47

Sagittarius, 89, 120

Saliva, 81

Salus (Hygeia), 95

Sanskrit, 22, 85

Satan, 6, 28, 61, 75

Scorpio, 88, 107, 116

Sedona, 229

Shades, 121, 123, 127–
   129, 182, 192, 195–196

Sheila-na-gig, 223

Shells, 24, 46, 81, 118,
   137, 163, 215, 223

Sky god, 38

Snake, 6, 27–29, 40, 58,
   78, 80, 95, 179

Solstice, 171

Spades, 89, 121

Spiral, 8, 27, 97, 168, 175

Spirit, 11, 13, 25, 27, 29,
   35, 45, 48, 55–56, 63,
   67, 77, 86, 93, 96, 99–
   100, 105, 143–145,
   147, 149–155, 158–
   162, 164–167, 170,

   175, 177, 179, 203–
   205, 209, 221–222,
   225, 230

Stars, 5, 76, 186

Swastika, 73

Sword, 74, 114, 123,
   213–214

Swords, 89, 120–122, 224

Tarot, 89, 105, 108,
   110–111, 113–122,
   213–217, 219

Tau cross, 74, 123, 213

Taurus, 88, 118

Taweret, 43

Teraphim, 45

Thor, 74, 114, 121, 224

Three petal flower, 76

Tints, 111, 116, 118,
   127–128, 192, 195

Tonantzin, 49

Triangle, 22, 33, 47, 68,
   76, 95, 98, 222–223

Udjat, 41

Uks Akka, 48

Umbilical cord, 28, 223,
   228

Uraeus, 80

V, 30–31, 223

Vanirs, 38

Venus, 88, 105, 116, 161,
   196

Vesta, 25–26, 44, 47, 70,
   78, 164, 172, 219, 229

Vitruvian man, 96

Vortex, 229

Vulva, 23–24, 68–69, 81, 223

Wands, 89, 113, 120–121, 219

Warrior, 37, 106, 114, 121–123, 213, 224

Water, 32, 49, 61, 79–80, 86, 88–90, 92–94, 96, 100, 105–109, 116, 118, 123–129, 131–132, 136–137, 139–140, 145, 154, 158, 161–163, 166–168, 170, 174–176, 178, 194, 196, 204, 206, 215–218, 231

Water birds, 79–80, 118, 215

Water snakes, 118, 215

White Lady of Ireland, 57

Womb, 22–26, 28, 30, 32–33, 40, 49, 53, 68–69, 76, 78, 222–224, 228, 233

Yggdrasill, 75

Zeus, 27, 39, 114, 121, 194, 224

Zigzag, 213, 223

Zodiac, 88, 107, 116, 118, 120–121

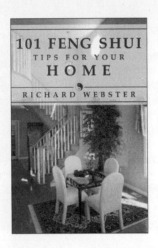

101 FENG SHUI TIPS FOR YOUR HOME

Richard Webster

For thousand of years, in the Far East, people have used feng shui to improve their home and family lives and live in harmony with the earth. Certainly, people who practice feng-shui achieve a deep contentment that is denied most others. They usually do well romantically and financially. Architects around the world are beginning to incorporate the concepts of feng shui into their designs. Even people like Donald Trump freely admit to using feng shui.

Now you can make subtle and inexpensive changes to your home that can literally transform your life. If you're in the market for a house, learn what to look for in room design, single level vs. split level, staircases, front door location, and more. If you want to improve upon your existing home, find out how its current design may be creating negative energy, and discover simple ways to remedy the situation without the cost of major renovations or remodeling.

1-7387-0498-9, 192 pp., 5¼ x 8, charts   **$9.95**

Spanish: **Feng shui para la casa**
1-56718-785-4, 176 pp., 5¼ x 8   **$7.95**

To Order, Call 1-877-NEW WRLD

Prices subject to change without notice.

FENG SHUI FOR YOUR APARTMENT

Richard Webster

Don't think that just because you live in an apartment complex, a one-room studio, or a tiny dormitory that you can't benefit from the ancient art of feng shui. You can indeed make subtle changes to your living area that will literally transform your life. Those who practice feng shui are noticing marked improvements in all areas—romantic, financial, career, family, health, even fame. This latest book in Richard Webster's Feng Shui series addresses the special ways that you can improve the harmony and balance in your apartment, at little or no expense.

Learn what to look for when selecting an apartment. Find out where your four positive and four negative locations are, and avoid pointing your bed toward the "disaster" location. Discover the best places for other furniture, and how to remedy negative areas with plants, mirrors, crystals, and wind chimes. You will also learn how to conduct a feng shui evaluation for others.

1-56718-794-3, 192 pp., 5¼ x 8, illus.   **$9.95**

Spanish: **Feng Shui para el apartamento**
1-56718-785-4, 160 pp., 5¼ x 8   **$7.95**

To Order, Call 1-877-NEW WRLD

Prices subject to change without notice.

THE WAY OF FOUR

Create Elemental Balance in Your Life

Deborah Lipp

Earth, Air, Fire, and Water; not only are these elements the building blocks of the universe, but also potent keys to heightened self-understanding. *The Way of Four* helps you determine which of the four elements are prominent and which are lacking in your world using a variety of custom-made quizzes. It includes a multitude of methods to incorporate and balance the elements in your environment, wardrobe, and even your perfume. This is a fun and valuable sourcebook for anyone seeking balance and beauty in a hectic world.

0-7387-0541-1, 336 pp., 7½ x 9⅛, illus. $17.95

THE MAGICAL HOUSEHOLD

Empower Your Home with Love, Protection, Health and Happiness

Scott Cunningham & David Harrington

Whether your home is a small apartment or a palatial mansion, you want it to be something special. Now it can be with *The Magical Household*. Learn how to make your home more than just a place to live. Turn it into a place of security, life, fun, and magic. Here you will not find the complex magic of the ceremonial magician. Rather, you will learn simple, quick, and effective magical spells that use nothing more than common items in your house: furniture, windows, doors, carpet, pets, etc. You will learn to take advantage of the intrinsic power and energy that is already in your home, waiting to be tapped. You will learn to make magic a part of your life. The result is a home that is safeguarded from harm and a place that will bring you happiness, health, and more.

0-87542-124-5, 208 pp., 5¼ x 8, illus. $9.95

FENG SHUI FOR BEGINNERS

Successful Living by Design

Richard Webster

Not advancing fast enough in your career? Maybe your desk is located in a "negative position." Wish you had a more peaceful family life? Hang a mirror in your dining room and watch what happens. Is money flowing out of your life rather than into it? You may want to look to the construction of your staircase!

For thousands of years, the ancient art of feng shui has helped people harness universal forces and lead lives rich in good health, wealth, and happiness. The basic techniques in *Feng Shui for Beginners* are very simple, and you can put them into place immediately in your home and work environments. Gain peace of mind, a quiet confidence, and turn adversity to your advantage with feng shui remedies.

1-56718-803-6, 240 pp., 5¼ x 8   **$12.95**

To Write to the Author

If you wish to contact the author or would like more information about this book, please write to the author in care of Llewellyn Worldwide and we will forward your request. Both the author and publisher appreciate hearing from you and learning of your enjoyment of this book and how it has helped you. Llewellyn Worldwide cannot guarantee that every letter written to the author can be answered, but all will be forwarded. Please write to:

Laurine Morrison Meyer

℅ Llewellyn Worldwide

P.O. Box 64383, Dept. 0-7387-0585-3

St. Paul, MN 55164-0383, U.S.A.

Please enclose a self-addressed stamped envelope for reply, or $1.00 to cover costs. If outside U.S.A., enclose international postal reply coupon.

Many of Llewellyn's authors have websites with additional information and resources. For more information, please visit our website at http://www.llewellyn.com.